Historical Association Studies

UXBRIDGE
COLLEGE

Historical Association Studies

General Editors: Muriel Chamberlain, H. T. Dickinson and Joe Smith

The Historical Association, founded in 1906, brings together people who share an interest in, and love for, the past. It aims to further the study and teaching of history at all levels: teacher and student, amateur and professional. This is one of over 100 publications available at preferential rates to members. Membership also includes journals at generous discounts and gives access to courses, conferences, tours and regional and local activities. Full details are available from The Secretary, The Historical Association, 59a Kennington Park Road, London SE11 4JH, telephone: 0171-735 3901.

British Politics since 1945

Second Edition

The Rise, Fall and Rebirth of Consensus

David Dutton

BLACKWELL
Publishers

Copyright © David Dutton 1991, 1997

The right of David Dutton to be identified as author of this work has been asserted in accordance with the Copyright, Designs and Patents Act 1988.

First published 1991
Second edition first published 1997

2 4 6 8 10 9 7 5 3 1

Blackwell Publishers Ltd
108 Cowley Road
Oxford OX4 1JF
UK

Blackwell Publishers Inc
350 Main Street
Malden, MA 02148
USA

British Library Cataloguing in Publication Data
A CIP catalogue record for this book is available from the British Library.

Library of Congress Cataloging-in-Publication Data
Dutton, David, 1947–
    British politics since 1945: the rise, fall, and rebirth of consensus/ David Dutton. — 2nd ed.
       p.   cm. — (Historical Association studies)
    Includes bibliographical references and index.
    ISBN 0-631-20320-6
    1. Great Britain—Politics and government—1945– I. Title.
    II. Series.
    DA589.7.D87   1997
    941.085—dc21   96–47026
                                                              CIP

Typeset in 11 on 13 pt Ehrhardt by Ace Filmsetting Ltd, Frome, Somerset
Printed in Great Britain by Hartnolls Limited, Bodmin, Cornwall

This book is printed on acid-free paper.

In Memory of Marion Eggington

Contents

Preface

The first damaging characteristic of our post-war politics has been that comparatively small changes in public opinion have led to violent switches in public policy of a kind not experienced by the multi-party democracies of Europe or the two-party democracy of the United States. (Steel, 1980, p. 159)

David Steel, then leader of the Liberal Party, wrote these words a decade and a half ago. His purpose, it must be said, was primarily political rather than historical. In a sympathetic analysis of the Lib–Lab pact of 1977–8, Steel sought to encourage acceptance of the idea that parties can and should co-operate with one another, as systems of proportional representation oblige them to do on the Continent. In a further condemnation of the pattern of post-war British politics, Steel went on:

Each government devotes much of its energy to undoing whatever its predecessor did, and nowadays the ink is not dry on a major Parliamentary Bill before Her Majesty's opposition is publicly pledged to repeal it. Each swing of the political pendulum threatens to take the country on yet more violently diverse directions to left and right. (Steel, 1980, p. 160)

Such a state of affairs does not encourage industry to take those long-term investment decisions which depend upon a stable environment. Two years later the former Labour cabinet minister, Roy Jenkins, put a similar point of view. Post-war Britain, he complained, had experienced 'too much short-term legislation, measures put on the statute book by one party in the almost certain knowledge that they will be reversed by the other' (Jenkins, 1982, p. 20). Neither comment is likely to survive the judgement of history. This short book aims to present a very different analysis of the reality of British politics after 1945, in which continuity rather than change was the order of the day. It is one which continues to have much significance for the contemporary political debate, though not in the sense that David Steel and Roy Jenkins implied.

It was the Labour prime minister, Harold Wilson, who once said that a week is a long time in politics. If so, the six years which have elapsed since the first edition of this book was written constitute a very long time in terms of the development of modern British politics and its historiography. In the intervening period the longest-serving prime minister of the twentieth century – and a key figure in the destruction of the post-war consensus – has been replaced, the Conservative Party has won, albeit narrowly, a fourth consecutive general election, yet the Labour Party seems now poised to return to power for the first time for nearly two decades. In the same period contemporary British history has become an ever more active area of academic enquiry and the available literature has grown enormously. The appearance of this second edition gives me the opportunity to take this recent historiography into account and to modify the argument originally presented, particularly in relation to the development of British politics during the Second World War. Nothing, however, has served to convince me that the basic argument put forward six years ago was unfounded. Indeed, I note that I then wrote that 'future historians may well write of the rise and fall and rebirth of consensus politics'. That argument can now be developed and, I think, sustained.

This book owes much to the scholarship of others. Some measure of this debt is indicated in the references. But to survey more than half a century of history in such a brief span necessitates considerable compression and omission. What is often a complex argument must, on occasions, be simplified more than is ideally desirable. The reader who wishes to take the subject further is urged to consult the works listed in the bibliography.

I must also acknowledge three particular debts: to Tessa Harvey at Blackwell Publishers for encouraging me to write this book; to Alison Bagnall for typing the whole work with accuracy and speed; and to my wife, Christine, for patience, encouragement and love.

David Dutton
Liverpool, 1996

Introduction

The post-war years in British politics have now become a legitimate area of academic historical enquiry. The thirty-year rule, which determines the availability of governmental records, means that, at the time of writing, the archives of the period up to 1965 are open to scholarly inspection. The fruits of research on these archives have worked their way into the published academic literature on the 1940s and 1950s. The 1960s are beginning to benefit from the same process. The publication of detailed diaries and memoirs by leading political figures, often after a much shorter interval of time than was thought seemly a couple of generations ago, has helped to fill many of the gaps of knowledge in the period still covered by the thirty-year rule. The use of new techniques, such as the interviewing of surviving participants, together with the undoubtedly closer contemporary scrutiny to which modern government is now subjected – notwithstanding the widely expressed concern about excessive secrecy in Whitehall – have further added to the availability of evidence for the contemporary British historian. The result has been the accumulation of a by now extensive literature covering the half-century since the end of the Second World War.

Furthermore, the passage of these years has been sufficient to enable historians to stand back and discern a distinct pattern of development over the period as a whole. It is that pattern which this book will attempt to explore. The argument is that for about a quarter of a century after the end of the Second World War there existed in this country, despite the superficial appearance of alternating governments of differing political complexion, a broad consensus between the two leading political parties. It is argued that this consensus, which came under increasing strain in the 1960s, broke down in the following decade and that the next fifteen or so years were characterized by a growing polarization of policies and ideals as between the Labour and Conservative Parties. Finally, there are good grounds for suggesting that the events of the recent past show that a new but very different consensus has come into being.

Any attempt to impose a structure or pattern on historical events is fraught with danger. It will be seen that the picture outlined above is open to detailed criticism. The development of British politics since the Second World War has not been quite as neat as this brief description would imply. The consensus bequeathed by the war was certainly far from complete; it never became total; important events foretelling its demise occurred as early as the 1950s; its destruction was not perhaps as complete as some commentators believed; scope for serious disagreement between the two major parties continues to exist, notwithstanding the emergence of the new consensus of the 1990s. Nevertheless, if critics set too high a requirement of internal consistency, they deny the validity of almost any conceptual approach to historical study.

It is, however, only right to acknowledge that some writers have denied the very existence of a post-war consensus. Their arguments merit consideration. Perhaps the most distinguished of these critics is the Labour historian, Ben Pimlott, for whom the whole idea is a 'mirage, an illusion which rapidly fades the closer one gets to it' (Pimlott, 1989, p. 13). Pimlott stresses that consensus means harmony and that it implies that its practitioners will frequently share a common purpose. Yet, he argues, the years after 1945 saw events shaped as much by dispute as by co-operation. Contemporary politicians did not feel themselves to be part of a consensus at the time, while the term 'Butskellism', so often employed to characterize the economic consensus of the 1950s, was regarded as a term of abuse, and brought credit to neither the Conservative,

Butler, nor the Socialist, Gaitskell. The theory, therefore, is a later invention, for the assumption of previous harmony was a way of contrasting the gulfs and divisions perceived to exist in the Thatcherite era. Pimlott further suggests that a middle ground consensus should have been conducive to the growth of a strong centre party, but in fact the years of supposed consensus saw the political centre – the Liberal Party – at its lowest ebb. He concludes, therefore, that 'consensus' is no more than a convenient piece of jargon 'to describe a time when we were all younger, more eager or more foolish' (Pimlott, 1988, p. 141).

It is possible to challenge Pimlott's analysis. His own definition of the idea of a consensus is somewhat tendentious and does not necessarily convey the meaning most usefully attributed to the concept in its political sense. Certainly it is not meant to suggest that there was a total absence of disputes between parties during the years when the consensus is thought to have prevailed. Contemporary observers are in any case not always the best judges of the nature of the party political divide at any given time. Divisions between Conservatives and Liberals before 1914 seemed very acute to contemporaries, but looked much less significant after 1918 when the two parties were confronted by the rapid advance of the Labour Party. A leading partisan of the earlier period could then comment:

> The questions which are coming up for settlement are not those which divided the parties in pre-war days but are economic and social questions challenging the very basis of our national life and industry upon which the older parties have always been agreed. (quoted in Dutton, 1985, p. 222)

The whole basis of British politics is adversarial in structure, right down to the procedures and formal customs of parliamentary debate. Even the physical lay-out of the House of Commons serves to pit government against opposition in a state of adversarial conflict, facing one another across an apparently unbridgeable divide. Not surprisingly, it is extremely rare for an MP to 'cross the floor' of the chamber, in other words to change his political allegiance and join the opposing camp, not least because the differences separating the two parties are perceived to be so great. The pattern common in Europe, where parties tend to sit as part of a continuous semi-circle, creates a very different impression. The evolution of modern British politics might have been very different if advantage had been taken of the destruction of the Commons chamber by Nazi bombs to change its architecture. When, however, Winston Churchill stood in the ruins at Westminster on the morning after the German attack, he made it clear that the new House would be rebuilt in every detail as a copy of the one which the Luftwaffe had destroyed.

Formal party political co-operation has been alien to the British system since 1945 except for the brief period of the Lib–Lab Pact in the late 1970s. The notion of 'confrontational' politics has enjoyed a recent vogue in describing the years of the Thatcher Government, but it is in fact an accurate description of the form (if not always the substance) of the modern British constitution as a whole. There is always a danger in such a system that observers – and even perhaps participants – will allow the rhetoric and propaganda of party political battle to conceal the essential underlying continuities of a largely bipartisan approach. The British system encourages opposition for opposition's sake, but the ritual of aggrieved indignation is often little more than the necessary accompaniment of a well-structured political game. The realization that a government possessing a majority in the House of Commons is unlikely to be defeated has merely added to the 'irresponsibility' of the opposition in opposing almost everything that government does. It does so in the knowledge that it will not in the immediate future be called upon to put in place an alternative policy. As Reginald Maudling pointed out in relation to the years 1966–70, parties in opposition tend to revert towards their own particular extreme. This, however, rarely tells us much about what they will do in office (Maudling, 1978, p. 141). In a two-party system there is, after all, little to be gained by an opposition party stressing its agreement with government policy. If an electorate is to be offered good reasons for rejecting a government and installing an alternative party in office, it is the differences – no matter how marginal or even exaggerated – which must be emphasized, rather than the points of agreement. Without differences being highlighted a general election becomes meaningless – simply a choice between more or less interchangeable sets of ministers. It was noticeable, for example, that the General Election of 1951 was among the most bitter and hard-fought of the post-war era, even though its outcome probably resulted in fewer changes of policy and direction than any other party political change-over of the same period.

Similar arguments apply to the position of the electorate. It is certainly true that the years of consensus were marked by a degree of consistent and passionate voter commitment unmatched in more recent times. Electors unhesitatingly proclaimed themselves Labour or Conservative in these years and the vast majority were unlikely ever to cross the dividing line between the two parties. Again, however, appearances may have been deceptive. 'Sandbagged in their electoral trenches', the voters of the 1950s and 1960s were not necessarily 'the anonymous infantry of two implacably opposed armies in an era of adversarial politics' (Pimlott, 1989, p. 13). We should be wary of attributing to the electorate either too high a degree of rationality in its voting decisions, or anything approaching a full knowledge of the party programmes on offer. Much of the strength of post-war party loyalty was founded upon deep-seated class consciousness and a family tradition of voting behaviour, both of which factors have diminished in importance in recent years.

Pimlott's idea that the 'consensus myth' is largely the product of a retrospective vision from the polarized era of Margaret Thatcher and Tony Benn is also open to question. Though Pimlott believes that the political orientation of those historians who subscribe to the theory of consensus may be significant – Thatcherites bolstering their convictions by reference to the mistaken compromises of earlier Conservative governments or Tory 'wets' and Labour Social Democrats hankering after a supposedly moderate past – it could well be that his own political convictions prevent him from seeing the Conservative Party as other than the hereditary enemy, pursuing fundamentally different objectives from his own. As Pimlott himself recognizes, the seminal work in the development of the consensus theory, Paul Addison's *The Road to 1945*, was published in 1975, the year in which Mrs Thatcher became leader of the Conservative Party but certainly before the concept of 'Thatcherism' had begun to impinge on the political consciousness.

Finally, Pimlott's argument that the existence of a consensus ought to have meant a strong centre party may be stood on its head. It was precisely the perceived moderation of the two leading parties which deprived the Liberals of any unique claim to occupy the centre ground in British politics. As early as 1947, one former Liberal noted 'a great deal of Liberal opinion . . . both in the Labour Party and in the Tory Party'. As a result, there had 'ceased to be any reason for a Liberal Party' (Lord Winster quoted in K. Young, 1980, p. 620). Not surprisingly, therefore, in the 1951 General Election the two main parties between them shared 96.8 per cent of the votes cast; in 1970 they still monopolized 91.5 per cent. It is surely instructive that the Liberal Party came close to disappearing within the Conservative ranks when Churchill formed his government in 1951, while just over a decade later there was serious talk of a realignment of the centre–left which might have seen Liberalism subsumed within the Labour Party of Gaitskell and Wilson. A Gallup Poll in September 1956 suggested that Liberal support had sunk to a derisory one per cent of those questioned. It was in fact the electorate's perception of the growing polarization of politics after about 1970, with the Conservatives moving to the right and Labour to the left, which left the centre ground vacant for a Liberal revival and even the temporary upsurge of a new force in the Social Democratic Party. At the 1983 General Election, with Labour and the Conservatives more clearly divided than at any time since before the war, the Liberal–SDP Alliance secured as much as 25.4 per cent of the popular vote.

Professor Pimlott is not alone in questioning the consensus theory. There are also historians who, while accepting the general validity of a post-war consensus, have challenged the conventional chronology of its birth. Kevin Jefferys disputes the idea that a consensus had been formed by the end of the Second World War. Party politics were, he asserts, alive and well beneath a surface veneer of war-time unity. When the Churchill Coalition came to an end in May 1945, it had not effected a fundamental change in the domestic basis of British politics. 'Conflict rather than consensus was once more the natural order' (Jefferys, 1987a, p. 14). In his detailed study of the war-time Labour Party, Stephen Brooke argues that the party used its membership of Churchill's Coalition from May 1940 to secure what was only the first phase in a much more radical agenda than their Conservative partners would have been prepared to accept and that there remained key issues of both social and economic policy which set the Labour Party apart. Labour's support for Churchill had a price and that price was socialism – not just a consensual middle ground (Brooke, 1992, p. 58). Both Brooke and Jefferys would therefore place the emergence of consensus no earlier than 1947, the product of an adjustment by both leading parties to post-war realities rather than the creation of the war itself. Peter Jenkins goes further, arguing that there never was a consensus (P. Jenkins, 1987, p. 4). He suggests that Britain suffered markedly from 'sharp and usually ideologically-inspired changes in direction' as a result of the alternation of Conservative and Labour governments after 1945 (P. Jenkins, 1987, p. 3). Yet, while he rejects the notion of consensus, Jenkins is ready somewhat paradoxically to concede that what he calls a post-war 'settlement' did grow out of the war years, which set out 'not only the framework but the agenda for post-war politics' (P. Jenkins, 1987, p. 5).

Roger Eatwell stresses that the level of consensus, either during the war or later, must not be overstated and that considerable ideological differences remained (Eatwell, 1979, p. 159). For Michael Fraser the reality is best expressed by seeing the Labour and Conservative Parties as two trains starting off from parallel platforms, running for a while along broadly parallel lines 'but always heading for very different destinations' (Hennessy and Seldon, 1987, p. 310). David Marquand accepts that the parties argued out their differences and settled governmental policies within a framework of common commitments and assumptions but regards 'consensus' as an imprecise term and warns that Labour and the Conservatives always differed profoundly about the details of policy, the source of political authority and the goals for which they were striving (Hennessy and Seldon, 1987, pp. 318–19). For Tony

Benn, anxious always to support his argument that Labour governments have failed to deliver their promised goal of a socialist society, the post-war or 'welfare-capitalist' consensus is merely one consensus to be set alongside that which existed after the formation of the National Government in 1931 and what he describes as the 'monetarist' consensus which began when the Labour government accepted the terms of the International Monetary Fund in 1976 (Hennessy and Seldon, 1987, p. 301).

These criticisms make it necessary to define precisely what is meant by the idea of a post-war consensus as the term will be used in this book. Indeed, it is clear that much of the debate as to whether a consensus ever existed has been conducted on the basis of the chosen, but differing, definitions of the historians concerned. Professor Pimlott, for example, insists that consensus is not achieved when people merely agree, 'but when they are happy agreeing . . . and leave few of their number outside the broad parameters of their agreement . . . Those who are part of it frequently share a purpose' (Pimlott, 1989, p. 12). At one level an important political consensus has existed in this country through-out the present century. There has long been a wide-ranging consensus as to the legitimacy of the state and its constitutional apparatus – something which was markedly lacking in, for example, the early years of the Third Republic in France. Furthermore, our modern party system could not have been developed without a basic agreement between the parties over the rules by which they compete for power and govern the country. An adversarial system could not in practice exist unless a fair measure of common ground is maintained between those parties which alternate in government. Indeed, it is basic to the successful functioning of a two-party system that the contenders for power should not be at completely opposite ends of a political spectrum. Any given period, moreover, tends to define for itself the range of policies which are capable of implementation, irrespective of the political colour of the party in power. Because political success within a democracy requires a party to appeal beyond its own natural constituency, there is an inherent tendency for all genuine aspirants for power to move towards the political centre. This was true even in the apparently polarized years between the two world wars. While Baldwin strove to contrast his Conservatives' 'national' appeal with Labour's, which he presented as 'sectional', Labour's primary concern in its two periods of power was to present itself as a moderate and responsible party of government. Keith Middlemas has traced in detail the evolution from the early years of the twentieth century of a consensus in which government 'moved from a position of facilitating to one of supporting economic change, and finally to direction – but only with the agreement of the governing institutions' including the trade unions and the employers' associations (Middlemas, 1979, p. 379). After 1939, the war-time alliance of government, unions and employers, designed in the first instance to facilitate victory over Hitler, formed the basis of a post-war corporate state. Finally, a tendency towards continuity and consensus is underpinned by the permanence of the British civil service whose inclination, it is often claimed, is to curb the wilder excesses of their political masters.

Yet after 1945 the concept of consensus came to mean rather more. The rest of this book will focus on the idea that after the end of the Second World War the political parties operated within a given framework, a set of generally accepted parameters in which certain key assumptions were shared and in which policy options were consequently limited. Disputes were less about absolutes than questions of 'more' or 'less'. In brief, on the domestic front these shared assumptions included the provision by government of a wide-ranging welfare state; the maintenance – with government as the accepted agent – of a high and stable level of employment; and the continuing presence of a mixed economy. Abroad the consensus embraced a commitment to the collective defence of the west in partnership with the United States and against the Soviet Union, while maintaining Britain's independent status as a great power; and the progressive evolution of the dependent Empire into the voluntary association of the Commonwealth.

Consensus is not meant to imply total agreement, nor an unspoken coalition of policy and intention. Nor should it be seen as a static body of agreed ideas. Key elements of the consensus, including attitudes towards the trade unions and the question of

European integration evolved over the period under review. The important point is that this process of evolution succeeded in carrying both parties towards the same basic conclusions. The consensus was never complete between the whole of the Labour and Conservative Parties. Each represented, as it always had, a broad spectrum of opinion. Labour contained both social democrats and an avowedly socialist left wing; Conservatism combined a collectivist, paternalistic strain with a free-market, libertarian right. The extreme poles of the two parties remained irreconcilable and could never be part of the consensus. What is important to note is that during the years under discussion it was the left wing of the Conservatives and the right of Labour which dominated their respective parties. The practical effect was a general convergence towards the centre ground of British politics. Bearing in mind what has been said already about the duty of opposition parties being to oppose, we may most clearly see the post-war consensus not in relation to the two political parties, nor even as between governments and oppositions, but in terms of the fundamental continuity between the governing elites of the two parties, alternating in power in succession to one another. It is in government that its practitioners learn that politics is indeed the art of the possible.

1

The Origins of the Consensus, 1940–5

For a long time – perhaps until the publication of Paul Addison's *The Road to 1945* – the Second World War was something of a backwater as far as British domestic political history was concerned. Attention focused, understandably enough, on the military and diplomatic history of these years, while the declaration of a party political truce as far as war-time by-elections were concerned and the formation of an all-party coalition in May 1940 gave the superficial impression that there were relatively few major domestic issues awaiting detailed historical attention. Yet changes in the political complexion of the country were clearly taking place, as the crushing defeat of Winston Churchill in the General Election of 1945 bears witness. The failure of Churchill, the great hero of the war effort, indeed the personification of the nation's resolve to resist Hitler's aggression, to cash in on the military victory secured in 1945 to the benefit of his own political party cannot simply be explained away as a delayed electoral condemnation of the failures, at home and abroad, of the Conservative-dominated National Government of the 1930s. Churchill's inability to repeat the experience of Lloyd George in 1918, and take the electorate by storm in 1945, can only be explained by fundamental changes in political attitudes during the war years themselves. It will be convenient to summarize the arguments of Addison and those who have followed his line before considering some of the important criticisms which have succeeded in modifying his original thesis.

Addison argued that these changes took place at both an intellectual and a popular level. Among the electorate as a whole, the sacrifices of the war years gave rise to heightened expectations about the securing of a better world when arms were finally laid down. In this respect the war was like its predecessor of 1914. But there were important differences. With government encouragement, the Second World War was seen as being fought for the benefit of the common man. It was a 'People's War' and it would be the people as a whole who would gain from ultimate victory. The ethos of the First World War had been altogether more conservative. In so far as the earlier war had promised improvements for the common man – 'a land fit for heroes to live in' – these had been largely disappointed. Yet, as the Second Word War progressed, there developed an overwhelming determination that such disappointments should not be repeated. The second war also disrupted civilian society, with all its deep-rooted class-based structures, to a far greater degree than had its predecessor, adding further to the egalitarian thrust which it carried forward. Some observers were not slow to recognize that, whatever it did to Britain's position in the international arena, the war might become a catalyst for major social and political change. Speaking in December 1939, the Conservative Anthony Eden declared that the war would 'bring about changes which may be fundamental and revolutionary in the economic and social life of this country' (quoted in Dutton, 1996, p. 250). From the Labour left Aneurin Bevan wrote at the beginning of 1940:

> War opens minds that were sealed, stimulates dormant intelligences and recruits into political controversy thousands who otherwise would remain in the political hinterland. It is with these new, eager virgin minds that Labour must concern itself if it is to breast the tides of war and emerge from it holding the leadership of the nation. (quoted in Campbell, 1987, p. 94)

Even though the war may have failed to kindle the revolutionary socialist fervour for which Bevan longed, its impact was nonetheless profound.

The war, argues Addison, inevitably changed people's perceptions of the proper role of government in society. The mobilization of a whole country for its supreme effort could not be, and was not, achieved using those techniques of *laissez-faire* and non-intervention which were still firmly entrenched in the governmental ethos of the 1930s. What government had claimed to be impossible only a few years earlier – namely to manage the economy successfully and eliminate unemployment – now seemed practical and realistic. It is also important to note that the new functions assumed by government during the war were widely judged to have been a success. It seemed remarkable that the unemployment which had been regarded as an intractable scourge of earlier years had been eliminated. Likewise the enormous industrial contribution to the salvation of the nation in the crisis of 1940 and to ultimate victory five years later seemed beyond dispute. Now it is true that the economic and industrial achievements of war-time Britain have been trenchantly and persuasively challenged by the historian Correlli Barnett. He argues that total employment in all sectors of the productive economy did not in fact rise during the war, but actually fell by about 1.6 million (C. Barnett, 1986, p. 260). Furthermore, British industry continued to display many of the long-term symptoms of decay which would come home to roost when the war was over. Yet as far as the present argument is concerned the contemporary perception is probably more important than the reality. The organization of the home front for war became something of a model for the reorganization of the peace.

The war thus aroused exaggerated beliefs in the power of the state to control the economy and to cure unemployment – beliefs that would not go away when peace returned. Centralized planning would be the panacea for the nation's post-war problems, including the creation of a better and fairer society, just as it had solved the problems thrown up by the war. For the man in the street this amounted to a gut feeling that government should intervene beneficially in areas from which it had previously been excluded. In June 1944, 68 per cent of those questioned agreed that post-war reconstruction should in the main be conducted under state control (Fielding, Thompson and Tiratsoo, 1995, p. 59). At Whitehall and

Westminster this feeling was increasingly underpinned by an intellectual acceptance of the ideas of the Cambridge economist, John Maynard Keynes. The war brought into the Civil Service large numbers of economists who had adopted Keynes's *General Theory of Employment, Interest and Money*, published in 1936, and who firmly believed that demand management of the economy was possible. In a remarkably short period of time Keynesian economics became the accepted orthodoxy. The concepts of a large public sector, high state spending and a generally active government had been legitimized.

Keynesian economics are of intrinsic importance to the post-war consensus and some attempt at definition must be made. The task is not easy. According to an old jibe, whenever five economists are gathered together, there will be six opinions and two of them will derive from Keynes (Peden, 1988, p. 35). Certainly Keynes himself recognized that economics deals with changing problems within a changing environment. His own ideas were steadily modified through the 1920s, 1930s and early 1940s. Yet their application to the policies of successive governments was most loudly proclaimed in the twenty-five years after Keynes's death in 1946. Broadly speaking, Keynesian economics implied that governments could and should accept permanent responsibility for aggregate demand in the economy, so as to ensure full employment without creating a vicious spiral of wage-price inflation. Keynes believed that the unfettered free market is economically inefficient and socially unjust and that government regulation through fiscal and monetary policies was necessary to ensure continuing growth. Perhaps his most novel idea was to argue that governments should be ready to borrow to finance expenditure when the economy was working at below full capacity (Peden, 1988, pp. 10–11).

According to Addison, by the end of 1940 a broad alliance, not party political in nature, was taking shape in favour of post-war social reform. What held it together was a belief in the state's capacity to reduce social injustice and, by expanding the economy, to create a better life for the whole population. The war was giving people a glimpse of a better and fairer way of doing things – and one which they had no wish to abandon when the war came to an end. It was not necessary to be a socialist to believe that the poverty and injustices of the 1920s and 1930s should be eliminated when peace returned. Allowing capitalism a free run and leaving the economy to be determined by the market had not, the experience of the inter-war years suggested, been conducive to prosperity for large sections of the population. Nor, of course, had it served to guarantee the survival of peace. A special edition of the magazine *Picture Post* in January 1941 showed how far the commitment to a planned society had taken root. In it the architect Maxwell Fry pronounced that when rebuilding began the new Britain would have to be planned. His message was echoed by the economist, Thomas Balogh, who promised that a planned economy would lead to full employment. To complete the vision A. D. Lindsay, the Master of Balliol, Julian Huxley, the scientist, and J. B. Priestley, the novelist and broadcaster, sketched their plans for education, health and leisure in post-war Britain. Priestley had already become a national figure as a result of his Sunday evening talks on the BBC. His central message was that there could be no going back to the social conditions of the 1930s (Addison, 1975, p. 118).

These developments need to be set against a background of important political changes which were taking place at the same time, though largely independently of them. In May 1940 Chamberlain's Conservative-dominated National Government fell from power to be replaced by a genuinely all-party coalition led by Winston Churchill. In this government most of the important posts on the domestic front were occupied by senior figures from the Labour Party. Indeed, with the exceptions of Anthony Eden and Churchill himself, the war failed to throw up many major new faces in the Conservative Party to replace that generation which had largely disappeared with Chamberlain as the 'Guilty Men' of the previous decade. Three key appointments should be noted. Clement Attlee, leader of the Labour Party, became Lord Privy Seal and later Deputy Prime Minister. In practice he increasingly emerged as the most powerful figure on the home front, allowing Churchill to concentrate on the diplomatic and military aspects of the war effort. In an inspired move Churchill appointed Ernest Bevin, General Secretary of the Transport and General Workers'

Union, as Minister of Labour. As such Bevin assumed crucial powers over the industrial labour force. Bevin brought the trade unions into a direct corporate relationship with the government to deal not only with industrial relations, but also with questions relating to the use of manpower, regional policy and welfare provision. During the war the unions developed a status in society that they had never previously enjoyed, and it was Bevin's presence which ensured that this new role should far outlast the ending of the war. 'This was no accidental shift of forces within the land, appreciated only long after the event. Bevin knew exactly what he was doing' (Hennessy, 1992, p. 69). Herbert Morrison had the chance to display his administrative skills as Minister of Supply and later as Home Secretary. These men emerged as respected and successful figures in the public mind and it was in the domestic ministries which they headed and the cabinet committees which they dominated that thought was given, at a governmental level, to the sort of society which should emerge when the war was over. The respective priorities of the two main parties within the government had important implications. While Churchill strove to win, Labour strove to win something beyond mere victory. This, of course, is a rather crude generalization. But it was also a clear perception in the eyes of the electorate.

On the whole the Coalition Cabinet functioned well. This is not to imply, of course, that there were no important disagreements within the government. But such differences of opinion are the very stuff of cabinet government, even in one of a single party. The glare of publicity and the propensity of recent cabinets to 'leak' information once regarded as confidential makes this abundantly clear to the contemporary observer, but it has always been the case. Yet an Australian observer of the Churchill government noted that 'practically all the Labour Ministers integrate loyally and helpfully with the Tories, particularly Bevin' (quoted in Pelling, 1984, p. 18). Attlee himself frequently emphasized the amount of common ground which existed between the major parties. This was not altogether surprising, for by 1940 the leading figures in the Labour Party had come a long way from the woolly idealism which had characterized Labour thinking during the early 1930s. Inspired by

Keynes's *General Theory*, it has been argued, they had come to re-examine the prospect of a Labour government trying to work within a healthy capitalist system. Their revolutionary days, if they had ever existed, were a thing of the past (Eatwell, 1979, p. 28).

Political developments in the government and changes in popular expectation among the nation at large came together as the Coalition itself helped to heighten public expectations about the post-war world with a series of officially sponsored blueprints for reconstruction. Of these the most important was undoubtedly the Beveridge Report of 1942. This milestone in social planning proposed that existing schemes of welfare support should be consolidated into a universal national scheme. Beveridge argued that the success of a future social security system would also involve the introduction of family allowances, the creation of a national health service and the maintenance of a high level of employment. This was not the blueprint for a socialist state. Indeed, it is worth pointing out that Beveridge himself was essentially a non-party figure, although he stood unsuccessfully as a Liberal in the General Election of 1945. The author of this great plan was perhaps more interested in social administration than social welfare and in institutions rather than people. The plan represented the coming together of existing pressures for a more progressive capitalism. Its timing was significant. Coming shortly after the victory at El Alamein, acceptance of Beveridge was almost synonymous with faith in victory and belief in a fair division of the fruits of that victory. Beveridge's vision, notes Kenneth Morgan, of a 'comprehensive social insurance system, binding private philanthropy and state provision into a uniform system, came close to embodying a national consensus about the purposes of the war' (Morgan, 1990, p. 14). It was some indication of Beveridge's impact that 635,000 copies of his report were eventually sold. In polls conducted after the publication of the report, 86 per cent of people said that it ought to be implemented and only 6 per cent not. The plan's impact and popular acclaim were such that the leading political parties had to accept it as the basis of the post-war society which one of them would have to build.

As Addison and others have shown, that acceptance was definite, if not of uniform intensity. On the Conservative benches there were certainly many who were as yet reluctant to envisage the sort of society which Beveridge proclaimed. The redistributive elements in Beveridge's proposals were widely disliked. More importantly, leading Conservatives in the government were hesitant on two grounds. Churchill in particular believed that one job should be tackled at a time. For the moment that job was to win the war. Discussions on the shape of post-war society were at best premature, but possibly also dangerous since they might divert attention from the immediate crisis, whose resolution was as yet by no means settled. If the military tide had begun to turn in Britain's favour after the defeats of earlier years, the transformation was far from complete. There was also a financial argument and the problem of raising public expectations which could not be met. Churchill had been in politics long enough to recall the mood of bitterness and disappointment when the 1920s failed to deliver the better world promised during the previous war. His Chancellor of the Exchequer, Kingsley Wood, warned that the Beveridge scheme, though largely based on contributions, would rely heavily on a deficiency grant from general taxation 'which will grow in the course of time to immense proportions' (quoted in C. Barnett, 1986, p. 47). The basic costs of post-war reconstruction might well pose an acute strain on the national economy without superimposing the burdens of an advanced scheme of social security. The Treasury was anxious that no particular commitments should be entered into until a clearer picture emerged of the country's likely financial burden as a whole (Jefferys, 1991, p. 119).

Such thinking determined the rather reserved stance adopted by the government when the House of Commons came to debate the Beveridge Plan in February 1943. From the front bench Kingsley Wood and John Anderson paid more attention to the report's costs than to its opportunities. It also explains why ninety-seven Labour members – virtually the whole of the party outside the Coalition Government – decided to defy their leadership and call for much earlier legislation than the government wanted. This outcome was doubly significant. On the one hand, there seems little doubt that both parties were now committed to a post-war welfare state. In the weeks following the parliamentary debate the prime minister sounded a more conciliatory note and began to reflect more actively upon the problems of post-war reconstruction. To reassure the public Churchill broadcast to the nation on 21 March 1943 and proclaimed that the members of the government were 'strong partisans of national compulsory insurance for all classes for all purposes from the cradle to the grave' (quoted in Addison, 1975, p. 227). In economic matters his tone seemed distinctly Keynesian. Unemployment would be prevented by government action to 'exercise a balancing influence upon development which can be turned on or off as circumstances require'. He even seemed ready to envisage an extended measure of state ownership. On the other hand, the public perception was that Labour was the party most likely to turn Beveridge's plans into post-war reality. The overall Conservative embrace of Beveridge seemed short on passion and conviction.

Such an analysis may not have been entirely fair. It is interesting that Beveridge himself had suggested that a Conservative government would be the best vehicle for carrying through his policies, while even Attlee suspected that the reason for Churchill's present caution was his determination to take personal credit for the implementation of the Beveridge proposals as the head of a post-war Conservative administration (K. Harris, 1982, p. 220). Some Tory ministers like Leo Amery had tried to get the government to adopt a more positive attitude to a report which he regarded as 'not only sound but essentially Conservative' (quoted in Addison, 1992, p. 367). Although Conservative enthusiasts for Beveridge were probably in a minority, a group of about three dozen MPs, mainly from the younger elements in the parliamentary party, formed the Tory Reform Committee led by Quintin Hogg and Lord Hinchingbrooke and called for the immediate creation of a Ministry of Social Security. This group kept up pressure on the party leadership to adopt a more positive attitude towards the Plan and enjoyed some success. The inclusion of two of its leading lights, Hogg and Peter Thorneycroft, as junior ministers in Churchill's Caretaker Government, formed after the break-up of the coalition in May 1945, perhaps indicated Churchill's grudging recognition that theirs' was the voice of the future. Labour's Hugh Dalton noted that the Tory Reform Committee 'would be quite prepared for a continuance of controls, for much state action and some state ownership' (Pimlott, 1986a, p. 597).

The Beveridge Report, Addison points out, was only the most important of a series of such planning documents produced during the years of the Churchill Coalition. A Cabinet Committee on Reconstruction was set up in 1943 and reached broad agreement on social security, education, child allowances and Keynesian budgetary management. White Papers soon followed. *Educational Reconstruction* was published in July 1943. It proposed a universal system of secondary education and prepared the way for the Education Act of 1944. Though recent research has shown that Conservative and Labour ministers were often at odds on points of detail, this should not blind us to the fundamental cross-party consensus which had emerged on questions of education. As *The Times* pointed out, during the two-day debate on the government's White Paper, 'not a single voice was raised in favour of holding up or whittling down any of the proposals for educational advance'. Later controversy on the issue of comprehensive schools can too easily obscure the widespread support, lasting until the 1960s, for the principles enshrined in Butler's act, including the segregation of eleven-year olds into grammar, secondary modern and technical education.

In February 1944 the government produced *A National Health Service*, which envisaged a free and comprehensive service to cover every branch of medicine. Then, almost as important as the Beveridge Report itself, came a White Paper on employment policy in May 1944. Its opening sentence would be engrained upon the hearts and indeed the manifestos of Conservative and Labour governments for the next thirty years. It would be the duty of governments to maintain 'a high and stable level of employment'. Some Tories were known to have considerable doubts about the feasibility of this far-reaching commitment and were concerned about the strain it would impose on other policies. The new party chairman, Ralph Assheton, fearing that the public had been promised more than could possibly be delivered, was among the sceptics. But once again there was a bipartisan consensus as far as the front benches of the two parties were concerned.

It was an agreement which greatly disturbed the socialist, Aneurin Bevan. In *Why not Trust the Tories?* (1944) Bevan condemned the White Paper as a surrender to market forces and capitalism. In Parliament he noted:

> The question of how the work of society is to be organized, how the income of society is to be distributed, to what extent the State is to intervene in the direction of economic affairs – all these are questions which first called this party into existence. They represent in themselves the main bone of contention between the main parties in the State. How on earth therefore can a Coalition Government pretend to approach these problems without the gravest sacrifice of principles? . . . if the implications of the White Paper are sound, there is no longer any justification for this Party existing at all.
> (quoted in Campbell, 1987, p. 130)

Bevan's comments are important. They emphasize that the new consensus – and the basis of the post-war Labour government's domestic policies – cannot really be described as socialist. It is perhaps best seen as the expression of a 'mildly interventionist social democracy', which would later be described as 'Butskellism'. It owed far more to Keynes than to Marx (Campbell, 1987, p. 144).

One policy area where inter-party differences certainly remained was the future ownership of British industry. The Conservatives set their faces against formal nationalization; by 1945 it was an important part of Labour's programme. Yet, even in this field, the party divisions should not perhaps be overstated. Though the word 'nationalization' remained anathema to them, many Conservatives, as well as leading industrialists, envisaged greater state regulation when the war was over. Coal provides an interesting example. The Coalition Government was committed to continuing state authority in its management, with reserve powers to effect compulsory amalgamations. The Tory Reform Committee went one step further, condemning the existing structure of the industry in 1944 and calling for a reduction in the number of companies to around fifty and the introduction of regional planning (Addison, 1985, p. 180).

Addison thus concludes that the general thrust of war-time developments had been in a leftward direction, towards a vaguely progressive future, but that it had been carried on a tide which had taken all parties along with it. As Attlee told Harold Laski in 1944, whichever party was in power after the war, it would have to work in a mixed economy (K. Harris, 1982, p. 254). The effective result, therefore, was to relocate the centre ground of British politics much further to the left than it had been in the 1930s. What might have appeared mildly revolutionary in 1939 had, only six years later, become an entirely natural evolution. Attlee was stunned at 'the extent to which what we cried in the wilderness five and twenty years ago has now become part of the assumptions of the ordinary man and woman' (quoted in Burridge, 1985, p. 140). But, as the moment approached for the electorate to install a party government in power once more, Labour was uniquely linked in the popular mind with the new social agenda that had emerged. By comparison many Conservatives seemed to have been driven helplessly along on the prevailing tide, 'apprehensively dropping anchor in strange Keynesian waters' (Addison, 1975, p. 166). As a result, 'when Labour swept to victory in 1945 the new consensus fell, like a branch of ripe plums, into the lap of Mr. Attlee' (Addison, 1975, p. 14).

The Road to 1945 is certainly a seminal work in the historiography of modern British politics. But, as Dennis Kavanagh has argued, 'no sooner does a thesis gain widespread acceptance than a challenge emerges' (Kavanagh, 1992, p. 175). In this case the challenge cannot be ignored since it has come from many directions and is based upon solid archival research. In the first place there are good grounds for questioning the extent to which either the Conservative or Labour Party was really committed to a consensus of the middle ground by the end of hostilities. In the case of the Tories the difficulty, as John Ramsden has shown, is to say precisely what war-time Conservative policy was. The party held no war-time conferences until 1943 and then no more until March 1945. Meanwhile, Churchill banned official policy statements which went beyond the plans of the coalition. By 1945, therefore, 'the Conservatives had established no policy identity that was separate from the all-party views of the government', making it 'extraordinarily difficult' to identify a distinct Tory position (Ramsden, 1995, p. 7). During the war the party's collective leadership completely disappeared while its structure, finances and organization virtually withered away (Ramsden, 1995, pp. 3–4). As Churchill projected himself as a national rather than a party figure, the Conservatives lacked a leader in the normal sense of the term. In such a situation the voices of pre-war Toryism were far from silenced. Conservative MPs reacted with suspicion to many measures of state regulation introduced by their own government. In December 1941 the backbench 1922 Committee protested against a policy of 'nationalization by stealth' and six months later orchestrated objections to what it claimed was a rigid and bureaucratic scheme of coal rationing (Ball, 1995, p. 101). Butler sensed a mood within the party that Beveridge was 'a sinister old man, who wishes to give away a great deal of other people's money' (Jefferys, 1991, p. 122). Churchill told Eden in 1944 that it was 'absolutely impossible' for him even to read the papers relating to his own government's plans for a national health service, let alone consider implementing them (Ramsden, 1995, p. 52). He even advised Henry Willink, Minister of Health in the Caretaker Government, not to announce such plans since they were as likely to lose votes as to gain them (Ramsden, 1995, p. 79). Though the Tory Reform Group may have been the voice of the future, it came no where near to capturing the party before the end of the war.

In the case of Labour it is far easier to define party policy, not least because the annual conference, sovereign in Labour's constitution, continued to meet throughout the war. The problem is that Labour policy was by no means identical to that of the 'consensus', if by that term we mean the policy of the coalition government. Stephen Brooke has shown that even over those measures commanding most agreement, profound differences of perception remained between Labour policy and coalition policy. Labour's aim was to get as much acceptable legislation as possible on to the statute book before the coalition came to an end. This would then provide the starting point for the much more radical agenda of a post-war majority Labour government. 'The national minimum, multilateral schools, a salaried medical profession and economic planning were key principles of policy setting Labour apart' (Brooke, 1992, p. 229). The innovations of Beveridge and Keynes were not ignored, but Labour's prevailing philosophy remained that of democratic socialism. Thus Keynesian demand management was integrated with ideas of socialist planning (Brooke, 1992, p. 232). According to this argument the existence of a coalition government blurred but did not remove deep-seated differences between the Conservative and Labour Parties, even in areas which saw apparent war-time agreement. Research has shown, for example, that R. A. Butler, the Conservative President of the Board of Education, and often singled out as an exemplar of progressive Toryism, was frequently at odds with his Labour deputy, James Chuter Ede (Jefferys, 1987a). Similarly, the Social Insurance White Paper of October 1944 received a fairly cool reception from the Labour Party and the trade unions, precisely because it failed to meet the demands of Labour policy. It could thus be suggested that such measures as were introduced or promised by the Coalition Government in the field of social and economic reconstruction represented the limit of inter-party agreement rather than the starting-point of a post-war consensus. More controversial matters were deliberately put to one side. As peace became a realistic prospect, the common ground began to look ever more fragile and there were clear signs of mounting controversy inside parliament and the government (Jefferys, 1991, ch 7). Thus, argues one historian, Labour's victory in the 1945 General Election presented the party not with the 'ripe plums' of consensus over industrial policy but with 'a rather acidic bunch of sour grapes' (Tiratsoo, 1991, p. 46).

A further line of attack has been developed against the Addison thesis in relation to the idea that the war-time consensus was carried along on a high tide of popular radicalism, the creation of egalitarian forces unleashed by the war. It is now clear that by no means everyone was consumed by a passionate evangelism born out of the social disruption and shared experiences of the Home Front. War-time surveys showed that schemes for social insurance and urban planning attracted something less than whole-hearted public endorsement (J. Harris, 1983). Many middle-class families, who opened their homes to working-class evacuees, were horrified by the uncouthness of their guests. Far from being broken down, class barriers and distinctions were, in many instances, merely confirmed. Air-raid shelters were as often indicative of continuing social divisions as they were the unlooked-for engineers of a more classless society. Profiteering abounded and a flourishing black market ensured that the introduction of rationing never quite guaranteed that equality of sacrifice of which the government spoke. There is evidence that as many voters were cynical about the whole political process as were enthused by the prospect of a 'new Jerusalem' dangled before them. After all, the scale of Labour's victory in 1945 can easily be exaggerated. Notwithstanding the distortions of the British electoral system which produced an overall parliamentary majority of 146 seats, Attlee's party managed to secure the support of little more than one in three of those entitled to vote. 'Idealism on a mass scale was prominent by its absence' (Fielding, 1992, p. 637). And if the popular mood was not as fully transformed by the experience of war as was once supposed, the same may well be true of the official mind. Several historians have cast doubt upon the reality of a Keynesian Revolution within the Whitehall elite (Rollings, 1988).

Where do these trenchant criticisms leave the idea that the wartime coalition gave rise to a new consensus about the role of the state in post-war society? As is often the case, it may be that the revisionist line is in danger of going too far. Addison never intended to suggest that the war witnessed the end of party conflict. Rather he argued that by 1945 the areas of agreement within the government were of more significance for the future development of British politics than were the party conflicts which undoubtedly persisted. Addison himself would now concede that *The Road to 1945* tended to exaggerate the extent to which 'middle opinion' had captured the two front benches by the end of the war (Addison, 1993, p. 93). He recognizes that the term 'consensus' could be misleading 'if taken to imply a society free of conflict or a natural harmony of opinion between the rank and file of the two main parties' and is happy to employ the phrase 'post-war settlement' to make this point clear (Hennessy and Seldon, 1987, p. 5). But

Addison's critics may have paid too much attention to dissent in the ranks of the Conservative and Labour Parties and too little to the very substantial harmony which the experience of coalition brought out of those who worked together within the government. As Rodney Lowe has pointed out, 'throughout the war there were conflicting pressures on party leaders to seek consensus and on backbenchers to reject it' (Lowe, 1990a, p. 161). Harold Laski, the Chairman of Labour's National Executive Committee, may have warned Attlee in June 1945 that the party could not accept the doctrine of continuity in foreign policy. But whether Attlee, after five years of working at Churchill's side, felt the same way is another matter. The testimony of well-placed contemporaries that the parties were moving closer together is difficult to ignore. Speculation was rife about a major political realignment emerging from the war. According to his private secretary, Anthony Eden, who was widely expected to lead the post-war Conservative Party, was so progressive and the Labour Party so conservative that 'the two could never make a two-party system between them' (Harvey, 1978, p. 152). In May 1943 Herbert Morrison discussed the concept of an 'electorally flexible coalition'. The idea was that the parties would go to the country committed to an agreed coalition programme but that they would be able to campaign against one another on the basis of party differences. The coalition, when reformed, would reflect the changed party balance in the House of Commons. At much the same time Bevin initiated discussions with Churchill about the terms upon which it might be possible to carry the coalition over into the years of peace (Addison, 1992, p. 370). These senior Labour figures would surely not have entertained such ideas had they perceived fundamental and irreconcilable divides between the two main parties. The safest conclusion is probably that while the consensus was by no means fully formed in 1945, its roots had been firmly planted.

At the defeat of Germany, Churchill gave to each of the party leaders within the war-time coalition the option of remaining in the government until the end of the Japanese war or else of withdrawing immediately so that an election could be held in July 1945. Attlee expressed a preference for an autumn election, an option which Churchill had not offered. Accordingly, the country went to the polls in July. Interestingly, R. A. Butler later recalled that he had wanted the coalition to continue at least until Japan had been beaten and 'preferably until the social reforms upon which we were in general agreement had been passed' (R. A. Butler, 1971, pp. 126–7).

Labour's overwhelming victory in the General Election of 1945 looks much less surprising after the passage of over half a century than it did at the time. In one sense there was little to choose between the two main parties – except, of course, that the one was led by the towering personality of Winston Churchill. Labour's manifesto proclaimed that it was a 'Socialist Party and proud of it', but at the same time it cautioned that socialism would not come overnight as the product of a weekend revolution and insisted that its members were 'practical-minded men and women'. Both parties shared – as did the Liberals – a common commitment to the programme of reconstruction worked out between 1942 and 1945. The Conservative manifesto, *Mr. Churchill's Declaration of Policy to the Electors*, pledged the party to implement Beveridge, to carry out the provisions of Butler's Education Act, to set up some sort of national health service, to embark on a major home-building programme and to maintain a high and stable level of employment. Labour, of course, was committed to these same goals and also to the traditionally Tory aim of ensuring that Britain remained a major world power, one of the Big Three with the United States and the Soviet Union, and at the head of the Empire. Public ownership was an area of dispute, but even here it was significant that Labour argued its case pragmatically, usually in terms of promoting greater industrial efficiency. Nationalization was not presented as an ideological crusade. This was not very different from the argument which the Conservative Harold Macmillan had used in his work *The Middle Way*, published in 1938. The Conservatives naturally stressed the virtues of free enterprise, but it was striking that they never quite ruled out the option of state intervention. Anthony Eden said that he would 'draw no rigid line. I would judge each on its merits' (quoted in Ramsden, 1995, p. 80). What was significant, however, was the scale of priority given to their various pledges by the two parties and the intensity with which they were presented to the electorate.

It was noticeable that statements on foreign policy came at the beginning of the Conservative manifesto and at the end of Labour's. But it was in the handling of the respective campaigns that the differences appeared most clearly to the electorate. Labour's focus was simply and emphatically upon the material needs of the ordinary family. Its message exuded moderation. Labour wanted to consolidate the achievements of the war-time consensus, to maintain the system of state planning which the war had created. Even Stephen Brooke concedes that for Labour in 1945 'socialism' meant only 'central economic planning, the retention of war-time controls and limited public ownership' (Brooke, 1995, p. 16). The Conservative campaign stressed the problems which still lay ahead and was often negative and divisive, particularly after Churchill entered the fray. Churchill insisted on giving priority to the on-going war against Japan before domestic reforms could be embarked upon. All Conservative candidates, but few from the Labour Party, stressed the need to maintain strong defences once the conflict was over. Butler later admitted that it would have been better if the Conservatives had not placed their commitment to post-war reconstruction a poor third behind the exploitation of Churchill's personality and a negative attack on the Labour Party (R. A. Butler, 1971, p. 128). Even Harold Macmillan from the Conservatives' left wing sounded cautious, with only guarded enthusiasm for the New Jerusalem ahead:

> In the realm of national economic planning we shall hold a wise balance between the field suited for private enterprise and that allocated for ownership or control . . . the Government will follow the national characteristic – a middle course avoiding equally the extreme of laissez-faire and that of collectivist control for its own sake (Horne, 1988, p. 284)

The fact was that progressive Tories had failed to persuade the majority of their colleagues to adopt the details of the war-time consensus as their electoral battle-cry. The coalition programme was accepted by many with only lukewarm commitment. 'If you do not give the people social reform,' Quintin Hogg had warned the House of Commons, 'they are going to give you social revolution' (quoted in Addison, 1975, p. 232). In practice the consequence was nearer to a political revolution, with the election of a majority Labour government for the first time in the country's history with a massive parliamentary majority of 146 seats over all other parties combined.

2

The Foundation of the Consensus, 1945–51

The Labour governments of 1945–51 have been well served by their historians (particularly Morgan, 1984; Pelling, 1984; K. Harris, 1982; Bullock,1983). Even so, they retain an enigmatic quality. Until fairly recent times there was at least a general recognition of the importance of their achievements, though the nature of those achievements was open to debate. Even Conservatives, notwithstanding a token genuflection to adversarial opposition, viewed these years with a grudging respect. Among Labour supporters in general there was none of the tendency, so marked after the later governments of 1964–70 and 1974–9, to denigrate the achievements of Attlee's administration or to distance themselves from its record. The two dominant Labour figures of the 1950s, Hugh Gaitskell on the right and Aneurin Bevan on the left, could both look back to the Attlee years with a sense of pride and satisfaction. But it remained open to question whether Labour partisans held the Attlee government in such esteem because it saw the only significant stride which Labour has ever taken towards the establishment of a socialist state, or because it marked Labour's firm entrenchment on the path of non-ideological social democracy. Yet in recent years a more critical commentary has become apparent. Tony Benn's assessment that 1945 marked the beginning of a 'welfare-capitalist consensus' has already been noted. Left-wing critics such as Ralph Miliband have seen the Attlee years as a period of wasted opportunity in which Labour opted for the paths of consensus at the expense of a root and branch transformation of British society. As a result, Labour's cautious reforms involved little redistribution of wealth, tied Britain to the capitalism of the United States and betrayed the radicalism of the electorate (Miliband, 1973, pp. 272–317). For the New Right Conservatives of the 1970s and 1980s, by contrast, 1945 inaugurated thirty years of collectivism and bureaucratic centralism. According to Correlli Barnett, Britain took a fateful wrong turning as the war came to a close, opting for the creation of a 'New Jerusalem', involving ultimately unsustainable levels of welfare provision, when what the country desperately needed was a programme of reinvestment in and modernization of its antiquated industrial infrastructure (C. Barnett, 1986). In this period the Conservative Party was shifted progressively in a socialistic direction by what Keith Joseph saw as a ratchet effect, while the country slid inexorably into deep decline before the rescue operation launched by Margaret Thatcher after 1979.

The character of the post-war Labour government is clearly of intrinsic importance to the argument of this book. For if the Attlee government really did mark the implementation of left-wing socialism, the thesis of a moderate post-war consensus growing out of the years of war falls to the ground. It will be argued that the major achievement of the Labour Party after 1945 was to complete and consolidate the work of the war-time coalition. The changes which the government introduced fell far short of a social or economic revolution. As in 1964 and 1974, though perhaps with greater competence, Labour set out to make the capitalist system work. The class structure of the country was hardly affected and there was no significant redistribution of the nation's wealth. Most of the government's measures were far less distasteful to the Conservative Party than was sometimes claimed. This is not to say that a Conservative government in 1945, especially one headed by Winston Churchill, would have pursued an almost identical course. Some clear differences would have been evident. But a Conservative government would have proceeded along very similar lines and operated within comparable parameters.

The moderation of the Labour government clearly requires some words of explanation. In the first place, its leadership was firmly planted in the centre, if not the right, of the Labour movement. The Big Four of 1945, Attlee (Prime Minister), Morrison (Lord President), Bevin (Foreign Secretary) and Dalton (Chancellor), were cautious and responsible politicians who had all served a governmental apprenticeship under Churchill during the war. Attlee was completely wedded to the parliamentary system and, whatever he may have believed earlier in his career, content to work within a mixed economy of reformed capitalism. If a genuinely socialist society was ever to be created, such an event lay far off in the future. The duration of the period of transition could not even be predicted. 'Have you read Karl Marx?' Attlee once asked a senior British diplomat. Sir William Hayter replied somewhat nervously that he had read only the potted version supplied by the Foreign Office. 'Haven't read a word of it myself,' retorted Attlee (Wyatt, 1977, p. 12). Though the parliament elected in 1945 contained much socialist idealism, the harsh practicalities of post-war reconstruction served greatly to temper unrealistic aspirations. By 1948 Harold Macmillan could note, with some concern for its impact on the Tory Party, that 'the Labour movement as a whole is turning towards the centre' (quoted in Horne, 1988, p. 300).

Beneath the Big Four many other leading ministers displayed similar moderation. At the Ministry of Defence, A. V. Alexander was almost an old-fashioned imperialist. The Home Secretary, Chuter Ede, exuded caution. Successive ministers of education, Ellen Wilkinson and George Tomlinson, were not likely to foster any sweeping changes. Plagued by ill-health, 'Red Ellen' had lost most of her 1930s radicalism. The left wing was represented in the cabinet by Aneurin Bevan and Emanuel Shinwell, although the latter could on occasions be remarkably conservative. Bevan had his hands full at the Ministry of Health and was effectively excluded from the determination of the main thrust of the government's programme. Shinwell, too, exerted little overall influence. 'The Attlee government', concludes its leading historian, 'does not emerge on the whole as a body of committed or instinctive radicals' (Morgan, 1984, p. 56). It was this government which, when confronted by a dock strike within weeks of taking office, re-enacted the detested Emergency Powers Act of 1920, with even Ernest Bevin, former General Secretary of the Transport and General Workers' Union, concurring.

Even had the leading members of the Labour government been more inclined to embark on a socialist crusade, the circumstances of the time would have conspired to constrain them. All governments are subject to, indeed sometimes prisoners of, a prevailing climate – political, diplomatic, economic and social – over which they have only limited control. This is particularly true in relation to overseas factors impinging upon Britain's position. But the post-war Labour government was more than usually restricted in its freedom of manoeuvre. The fundamental fact of life in 1945 was that Britain was all but bankrupt. During the course of the war the country had lost about a quarter of its entire national wealth. The financial and economic legacy of the struggle against Hitler was almost unendurable. The combination of lost overseas assets, a massive trade imbalance, lost markets, a shortage of raw materials and an enormous dollar deficit would take many years to overcome. The government, presented by Keynes with the grim realities of the situation in its first week in office, made the acquisition of a loan from the United States in the order of five billion dollars its first priority. Though not all realized it at the time, the basic pattern of the government's affairs had thus been fixed.

Labour's six years in power were marked by continuous domestic economic difficulties. In addition, the government was constantly mindful of the need to avoid damaging the country's exports, to maintain confidence in sterling and not to endanger continued American generosity in terms of loans and aid. The last factor was perhaps the most important of all. Without the inflow of American cash Britain would have faced conditions of extreme austerity and the most cherished of Labour's designs, the welfare state, would scarcely have got off the ground. The party's left wing, largely removed from the responsible seats of power, often overestimated the relatively narrow scope of choice open to the government.

This situation determined Labour's approach to the general management of the national economy. The environment of internal and external crises ruled out any real prospect of socialist planning of the country's production. There were some moves early on, especially in the Steering Committee on Economic Policy, towards long-term macro-economic planning, but these were short-lived and did not really survive the end of Dalton's Chancellorship in 1947. According to his biographer, Dalton's resignation symbolized 'the end of the radical phase and the start of a period of compromise and consolidation' (Pimlott, 1985, p. 536). Even under Dalton, Labour's efforts to plan the private sector via the Treasury and the Board of Trade were half-hearted and not particularly successful. Genuine efforts at planning were restricted to coping with scarcity. 'There was no intention at any level to operate a more ambitious definition of planning for economic regeneration' (Hennessy, 1992, p. 434). According to the government's Chief Planning Officer, policy amounted to 'a mixture of physical controls, nationalisation and exhortation, laced with a dash of Keynesianism and a liberal dose of wishful thinking' (Hennessy, 1992, p. 212). The public ethic of 1945–7, concludes Kenneth Morgan, 'was more a matter of exhortation and an assumed public morality than of concerted planning' (Morgan, 1990, p. 67). From 1948 the physical controls on investment and the use of raw materials were progressively dismantled. Pragmatism now became the hallmark of Labour's domestic policy (Jefferys, 1992, p. 42).

Sir Stafford Cripps, Chancellor from 1947 to 1950, has been described as beginning the long reign of Keynesians at 11 Downing Street which lasted perhaps until 1979 (Morgan, 1984, p. 364). Despite his left-wing past Cripps had now become a committed supporter of the mixed economy. Under him, and much to the annoyance of Labour's Left, the vague commitment to centralized economic planning was abandoned, apart from the setting of optimistic targets. An economic strategy based upon demand management by fiscal and budgetary means took its place which would dominate the Treasury's thinking until the 1970s. The rise of young Keynesian economists such as Douglas Jay and Hugh Gaitskell within the ranks of the government confirmed the change of course. As a Treasury mandarin of the time commented: 'The last government adopted in 1947 and 1948 a revolution in British

practice, when they took responsibility for maintaining full employment but avoiding inflation' (quoted in Morgan, 1984, p. 364).
Symbolic of the change was the so-called 'bonfire of controls'
inaugurated by Harold Wilson, the President of the Board of Trade,
in November 1948. Though the Conservatives would later be
elected on the slogan of 'setting the people free', most of the work
had already been done for them before they entered office. It made
sense for the Tories to use this sort of rhetoric since the persistence
of rationing and controls was giving rise to a reaction in favour of
deregulation. But this was a trend to which the Labour government
was already responding. By the time of Cripps's last budget in 1950
The Times could comment that Labour had finally made the
transition from idealistic theory to common sense. The actual
experience of government had proved 'a graveyard of doctrine' and,
in an important sense, a barrier had been erected between the
Labour Party and the economic theories of Marxism (K. Harris,
1982, p. 452). By the end of the 1940s, socialist critics such as G.
D. H. Cole were complaining of the apparent continuity between
the policies of the war-time coalition and those of the post-war
Labour government (Brooke, 1992, p. 4).

If one socialist beacon shone forth from the Labour government's
otherwise orthodox economic record, it was surely its policy of
nationalization. Here was a practical response to the commitment
entered into through its socialist constitution back in 1918. Yet a
number of qualifications must be made. In the first place, the general
concept of public ownership was not new, as the establishment of the
Port of London Authority in 1909 and the Central Electricity Board
and the British Broadcasting Corporation in 1926 bear witness. The
war, of course, had provided many examples of governmental control
of industry, and the widespread readiness to see such practices
continue into the peace showed that nationalization was not
primarily envisaged as dogmatic socialism. Many industrialists and
managers, traditional supporters of the Conservative Party, were
convinced by the experience of the war that a measure of state control
was necessary. They were ready to support the compulsory
reorganization of certain key industries, particularly in fuel and
transport, which would be vital for post-war reconstruction.

Labour's nationalization programme was largely the responsibility of Herbert Morrison and it is striking that he sought to justify each measure on its merits as a way of improving the efficiency and usefulness of the industry concerned. It was in these terms that nationalization was presented in Labour's 1945 manifesto, *Let us Face the Future*. Indeed, this document preferred to use the term 'public ownership' rather than 'nationalization'. Thus an economic rather than a political or social justification predominated in Labour's rhetoric. This fact determined the rather narrow range of industries which came into public ownership during the lifetime of the Labour government. The chief elements in Labour's programme were the Bank of England (1946), coal (1947), electricity (1948), gas (1948) and the railways (1948). Nor did Morrison envisage the programme of 1945 as merely the beginning of a longer-term or more wide-ranging assault on private industry. It is striking that the policy document *Labour Believes in Britain*, published in 1949, marked 'an evident downgrading of the standing of nationalisation in Labour's future priorities' (Morgan, 1984, p. 123). Thus the industries encompassed in Labour's vision were 'either public utilities or ailing concerns of little value to their owners and no interest to other capitalists' (Addison, 1975, p. 273). The main exception was the commitment to nationalize the steel industry. Significantly, steel had been included in Labour's shopping list at the insistence of the party conference in 1944, but against the advice of Morrison and Arthur Greenwood. This was the one case where Labour did seem ready to tackle 'the commanding heights of the economy'. Its inclusion was more overtly ideological than any other nationalization measure which Labour undertook.

Most of the private sector of British industry, particularly its profitable parts, remained untouched by Labour's plans. The most that the government aspired to was a loose partnership with industry – one in which the forces of capital and the market would remain supreme. The form generally taken by those industries which were nationalized is also worthy of note. It was that of the public corporation. Most of the new state-run industries were organized very much as they had been before, though on a larger scale. This involved the creation of no new relationship between capital and labour. There was little in the way of worker participation in the running of the company. All that effectively happened was that the state bought out the existing ownership while allowing the existing management to remain in its place. For its chairmen and governors the government looked to capitalists recruited from the private sector. The one exception was Lord Citrine, the former General Secretary of the TUC, who was now appointed to the British Electricity Authority. If this amounted to a socialist transformation, it was one which largely passed the average employee by.

These factors determined the reaction of the Conservative Opposition to Labour's programme. Significantly, Harold Macmillan once commented of Morrison that on the question of the nationalization of public utilities, railways and the coal industry, 'our views were not very far apart' (Horne, 1988, p. 258). Less progressive Tories than Macmillan no doubt felt a gut revulsion against the whole concept, but the behaviour of the Opposition front bench is instructive. Attlee later recalled that, with the exception of steel, there was 'not much real opposition to our nationalization policy' (Attlee, 1954, p. 165). Labour's first measure, the nationalization of the Bank of England, was carried without controversy. Churchill said that the measure did not involve 'any issue of principle'. Conservatives were relieved that Labour was not proposing to shackle the main clearing banks or to try to control the movement of capital. The case of coal was not dissimilar. War-time plans had envisaged some form of state control. The Reid Committee, appointed by the Coalition Government to examine the technical efficiency of British coal-mining, had reported in the last days of the war that the necessary changes could not take place 'unless the conflicting interests of the individual colliery companies were merged together into one compact and unified command of manageable size' (Chester, 1975, pp. 11–12). Though the Conservatives voted against the second reading of the bill, neither Churchill nor Eden offered more than token resistance in the Commons debate. Eden seized upon a speech of Morrison's in which the latter had argued that particular acts of nationalization were needed 'in the public interest', rather than for ideological reasons.

Eden now retorted, 'Let the argument be directed to the merits, and let the test be the public interest' (Ramsden, 1995, p. 187).

On other measures the Conservatives put up a stiffer fight. The Transport Bill, covering road haulage, was vigorously opposed, as was that dealing with electricity. Though the Conservatives had accepted the report of the Heyworth Committee, recommending the public ownership of the gas industry, this did not stop them from putting down more than 800 amendments before the government's bill received the royal assent in July 1948. In part this reflected little more than a recovery of Tory morale from the low point of 1945. Even so, Labour's legislation was reformist and, in the circumstances of post-war Britain, not particularly controversial. The impression is that the Opposition's resistance was largely tactical and that, had they been in power in these years, some form of public ownership might still have resulted.

In the case of the steel industry it was a different story, and it is noticeable that opponents of the consensus thesis often fall back on this example to support their case. 'The sheer ferocity of the steel debates of 1949–53,' writes John Ramsden, 'rather belies the idea of it being only a mock-contest.' Contemporaries 'saw a real divide between the parties over public ownership and not just a matter of emphasis' (Ramsden, 1995, p. 9). It is certainly true that over the period covered by this book steel was nationalized twice and denationalized (or privatized) twice. But three additional factors are important. First, here Labour did seem to be crossing the important frontier between nationalization as a practical economic measure and nationalization as part of an overtly political objective. Second, the Labour leadership itself seemed unenthusiastic about its own proposals. The steel nationalization bill proposed to take over companies *en bloc* without reorganization or restructuring, thus making it relatively easy for a future Conservative government to denationalize the industry. And third, the timetable of Labour's crowded legislative programme ensured that steel became an election issue, where the Conservatives could call on the support of their traditional allies in industry and commerce, as the parliament of 1945 inexorably ran its course.

If its nationalization programme will not wholly sustain its socialist credentials, the left-wing admirers of the 1945 government would probably point to its social policy, and particularly the setting up of the National Health Service in 1948, as corroborative evidence. Once again, however, it is clear that, at least in general terms, much of the groundwork had been carried out by Churchill's coalition. This was particularly the case in relation to James Griffiths's National Insurance Bill, although the Labour cabinet did decide to increase the scale of benefits previously proposed. Significantly, it was Churchill's Caretaker Government which had put the Family Allowances Bill on the statute book in June 1945. Based on the principle of universality, that bill, writes Peter Hennessy, 'was both a symbol and a pioneer of a new way of giving and receiving' (Hennessy, 1992, p. 129). Not surprisingly, the Conservative Opposition decided not to oppose Griffiths's bill on second or third reading in the Commons, and the parliamentary guillotine was not required to ensure its quick passage. It was noticeable that the whole scheme was established on a sound actuarial basis. Benefits were not linked to the cost of living and any individual was free to take out additional cover from private insurance companies.

Only in the area of the National Health Service is there really scope for suggesting that Labour's enactments went significantly further than a Conservative government would have progressed. The Health Service is widely seen as a legislative memorial to Aneurin Bevan, the most avowedly socialist member of Attlee's cabinet. According to Kenneth Morgan, 'the National Health Service is a prime exhibit in illustrating the danger of making too much of the continuity between the social consensus of the war years and the post-war Labour welfare state' (Morgan, 1984, p. 154). He argues that the ideas drawn up in 1944 by Henry Willink, Churchill's Minister of Health, fell short of Bevan's proposals in certain key areas, especially hospitals and health centres, and that a Conservative government would have introduced a much less ambitious scheme. It is, of course, impossible to prove what a post-war Conservative government would or would not have done. But other historians have been rather less convinced of the uniqueness of Bevan's achievement. Addison asserts that 'it is as certain as anything can be that a post-war Conservative government would have [established], in some form, a national health service' (Hennessy and Seldon, 1987, p. 14). As Churchill had told the Royal College of Physicians in March 1944, 'our policy is to create a national health service in order to ensure that everyone in the country, irrespective of means, age, sex, or occupation, shall have equal opportunities to benefit from the best and most up-to-date medical services available' (quoted in Addison, 1992, p. 374). It should be stressed that the basic idea of a comprehensive national health service was not new. Inter-war reports, such as the Dawson Report of 1920 and the Royal Commission on National Health Insurance in 1926, had pointed towards such a conclusion. It became a definite prospect with the acceptance of 'Assumption B' of the Beveridge Report in 1943. But, even before Beveridge, discussions had been going on inside the Ministry of Health, headed first by the Liberal National Ernest Brown, and then the Conservative, Willink. All political parties accepted that the post-war parliament, whatever its political complexion, would introduce some scheme of comprehensive health cover. The British Medical Association itself was putting forward proposals, as were the leading medical journals, including *The Lancet*.

Bevan himself seems to have exaggerated his own achievement. His abrasive style and confrontational tactics were such as to create the impression of an heroic struggle, successfully carried out in the face of adversity and opposition. Bevan strove to make as much party political capital out of his creation as he possibly could. But the minister's greatest battle was fought less with the Conservative Opposition than with the British Medical Association, though the Conservatives took up the doctors' cause in the House of Commons. The Tories' opposition was 'largely based on tactics and administrative detail rather than principled hostility to the idea of an expanding state and a client citizenry' (Morgan, 1990, p. 32). It is instructive that when Attlee proposed to make a broadcast in which he would describe the NHS as a national achievement to which all parties had contributed, Bevan objected forcefully. Just before the Health Service came into operation Bevan made his notorious speech in Manchester in which he described the Tories as 'lower than vermin'. 'It seems clear', writes his latest biographer, 'that Bevan privately welcomed . . . the B.M.A.'s help in making the N.H.S. appear a more socialist measure than it really was' (Campbell, 1987, p. 179). Disappointed at the lack of socialist content in the rest of the government's policies, Bevan took comfort in the free Health Service, 'elevated into the touchstone of socialism' (Campbell, 1987, p. 149). The Labour spokesman in the House of Lords probably gave a fairer analysis. The NHS Bill, he said, 'was not the product of any single party or any single government. It was in fact the outcome of a concerted effort, extending over a long period of years, and involving doctors, laymen and government, to improve the efficiency of our medical services, and to make them more easily accessible to the public' (quoted in Letwin, 1992, p. 203).

Most of the rest of Labour's domestic programme followed the same pattern. Education may be taken as an example, since it was an important element in the war-time consensus, while becoming a matter of inter-party dispute in the 1960s. The main task of Labour's minister, Ellen Wilkinson, was to put into operation a piece of legislation which was already on the statute book – Butler's Act of 1944. Her aim was to make secondary modern schools as good as grammar schools, but the pursuit of equality did not to her imply treating different people in the same way. As a grammar school product herself, and far less radical in her outlook than she had been in the 1930s, Wilkinson had little sympathy for the view which enjoyed some support in left-wing circles, that the Butler scheme was socially and educationally divisive. Her successor from 1947, George Tomlinson, made no fundamental change in the thrust of government policy. The private sector persisted, allowing prosperous parents a choice of schools denied to those lower down the social ladder and, in the eyes of many, perpetuating distinctions based on social class.

The realm of foreign policy provides perhaps the clearest evidence of the centrist position occupied by Attlee's government. Paradoxically this was an area where, despite a long tradition of bipartisanship, Labour activists expected that the policies to be pursued by their government would be distinctly different from those which could be expected from a Conservative administration. The notion of a socialist foreign policy was in common currency in 1945, although precisely what it would mean in practice was not clear. Earlier Labour governments could be forgiven for their failure to adopt a distinctive approach because of their lack of a parliamentary majority, but no such impediment existed now. Whatever a socialist foreign policy might entail, it was certain that the Labour government could be expected to build on the close war-time ties with the Soviet Union, whose standing in popular esteem, particularly as a result of the heroic exploits of the Red Army, had never been higher throughout that regime's history. For many years to come Labour activists would recall Ernest Bevin's promise given during the election campaign that 'left could speak with left' in comradeship and confidence, even though Bevin had probably had Anglo-French rather than Anglo-Soviet relations in mind.

Yet, as Denis Healey wrote in 1952, 'an understanding of the power element in politics is the first necessity for a sound foreign policy' (quoted in James, 1972, p. 59). Diplomacy is a far harder field than domestic politics for any given government to chart a distinctive course in, because more of the basic determinants lie outside the control of so-called policy makers. This was particularly true in 1945. The pattern of war-time great power relations unfolded inexorably towards the new conflict of the cold war, a conflict in which Britain's position was never seriously in doubt, if for no other reason than her total dependence on American financial support. Ernest Bevin, a surprise appointment to the Foreign Office (Dalton had expected to get the job), exercised a dominant and all-important influence over British diplomacy for the greater party of the duration of the Attlee government, and succeeded in laying down a framework of policy which would form the basis of Britain's overseas relations under successive governments of differing political complexions for many years to come.

As soon as he had taken up the seals of office Bevin was thrown into the fray of great power relations as he and Attlee travelled to Potsdam to take over the seats of Eden and Churchill at the resumed Big Three Conference. The observation of the American Secretary of State, James Byrnes, is revealing: 'Britain's stand on the issues before the conference was not altered in the slightest, so far as we could discern, by the replacement of Mr. Churchill and Mr. Eden by Mr. Attlee and Mr. Bevin' (Byrnes, 1947, p. 79). This was not altogether surprising. Bevin was a hard-headed politician, whose earlier trade union career had left him with no love of Communism. Perhaps his major political contribution of the 1930s had been to help disabuse the Labour Party of its more idealistic fantasies and anchor its thinking firmly in the real world. During the war he had no doubt soaked up many of Churchill's foreign policy attitudes and beliefs, including his fundamental mistrust of Soviet Russia. According to Alan Bullock, it was the experience of two years' preparatory discussion of the post-war international settlement within Churchill's War Cabinet 'which shaped the Labour leaders' and particularly Bevin's and Attlee's views when they came to formulate the policy of a Labour Government' (Bullock, 1983, p. 66). Bevin's eminently practical attitude is well illustrated in this judgement of Molotov, his Soviet opposite number: 'If you treated him badly he made the most of his grievance and if you treated him well he only put up his price and abused you next day' (quoted in Sked and Cook, 1979, p. 54).

If Bevin had nurtured any fond hopes of co-operating success-fully with Stalin's Russia, these could not have lasted long. Indeed, recent research suggests that Bevin's greatest achievement was to open the eyes of the United States to the reality of the Soviet menace and to secure an American protective role in recognition of Britain's incapacity, standing alone, to shoulder the burden of anti-Soviet defence (Bullock, 1983, pp. 839–48). By the time of the Foreign Ministers' Conference in Moscow in March 1947, Bevin and his American opposite number, George Marshall, were in substantial agreement on all important questions. Thereafter the government's absorption into the 'economic, political and military orbit of the United States became ever more explicit', particularly after the Czech coup of February 1948 and the Berlin blockade four months later (Morgan, 1984, p. 277).

The consistently anti-Soviet stance in Bevin's foreign policy provoked more disquiet on Labour's benches than any other aspect of the government's policies and programme. The foreign policy amendment to the Address in November 1946 was the most striking example, and the emergence in the summer of 1947 of the 'Keep Left' group of fifteen left-wing MPs a poignant reminder, of the extent to which the Foreign Secretary was deviating from the paths of true socialism. 'It seems quite remarkable', recalled Ian Mikardo, one of the group's leading lights, 'that the 1945 hope and expectation of a great leap towards a socialist Britain should have faded so fast' (Mikardo, 1988, p. 101). But, in the face of repeated illustrations of Soviet aggression and treachery, it became difficult for all but the most overt fellow-travellers in Labour's ranks to hold out against the logic of Bevin's stance. 'Keep Left' called upon the government to 'review and recast its conduct of international affairs so as to . . . provide a democratic and socialist alternative to an otherwise inevitable conflict between American Capitalism and Soviet Communism'. But it was an unrealistic aspiration. By early 1947 the vast majority of Labour MPs accepted Bevin's diagnosis of irreconcilable Soviet hostility towards the United Kingdom. As one diplomat noted of a foreign affairs debate in June 1947, 'the whole House was soberly anti-Russian' (quoted in Morgan, 1984, p. 261).

It is striking how many momentous decisions were taken during Bevin's Foreign Secretaryship. This was the government which determined in January 1947, albeit without full cabinet consultation, that Britain should build its own atomic bomb. Bevin's personal view of the bomb's importance is revealing. 'We have got to have this thing over here whatever it costs . . . We've got to have the bloody Union Jack flying on top of it' (quoted in Bullock, 1983, p. 352). Two months later a National Service Bill was introduced to provide for peace-time conscription, while during the Berlin airlift of 1948 the government agreed to the siting of long-range American atomic bombers on British soil. Then in 1949 Britain became a founder member of NATO – very much a personal achievement of Ernest Bevin and, from that day to this, the basis of the country's foreign and defence policies. In 1950 Britain proved a loyal ally of the United States in the Korean War.

In the circumstances it was scarcely surprising that Bevin's foreign policy proved largely uncontentious as far as the Conservative Opposition was concerned. Bevin and Eden, his Conservative predecessor, got on well together and continued to engage in private consultation after the end of the coalition. 'I would publicly have agreed with him more', Eden later wrote, 'if I had not been anxious to embarrass him less' (Eden, 1960, p. 5). It was certainly true that the repeated endorsement of a Labour Foreign Secretary's policies from the parliamentary Opposition and the right-wing press was galling for left-wingers. Butler, too, recorded that 'on the major public issues arising from the cold war there was rarely much between us save a difference of emphasis or detail' (R. A. Butler, 1971, p. 131). Talks even took place between Labour and Conservative front-benchers on defence matters in the summer of 1949.

The foreign policy consensus extended beyond the central questions of Anglo-American and Anglo-Soviet relations. Fundamental to the Labour government's approach was its acceptance as axiomatic that Britain remained one of the world's great powers. As Bevin declared in May 1947, 'I am not aware of any suggestion, seriously advanced, that, by a sudden stroke of fate, as it were, we have overnight ceased to be a great Power' (quoted in Porter, 1994, p. 256). Of the decision to construct an atomic bomb, Margaret Gowing has written that it was a response to 'a feeling that Britain as a great power must acquire all major new weapons, a feeling that atomic weapons were a manifestation of the scientific and techno- logical superiority on which Britain's strength . . . must depend' (Gowing, 1974, p. 184). The government's record in extricating Britain from the increasingly hopeless obligations of the Palestine mandate and from imperial entrenchment in the Indian sub- continent should not obscure Bevin's determination to maintain Britain's power and influence in many other parts of the world, including the Eastern Mediterranean and the Middle East. After the granting of independence to India, Bevin could still tell the Commons that 'His Majesty's Government do not accept the view . . . that we have ceased to be a great power, or the contention that we have ceased to play that role' (quoted in Sked and Cook, 1979, p. 69). Not surprisingly, defence expenditure remained at a high level throughout the life of the government. By 1951 Britain was even committed to a higher *per capita* defence expenditure than the United States (Morgan, 1984, p. 279).

Labour's convictions about Britain's great power status determined its attitude towards two other major questions of overseas policy, the future of the Empire and the first tentative steps towards European integration. The granting of independence to India in 1947 was, of course, the most important element of Labour's imperial policy. Churchill's opposition to this move is well known and it would be wrong to deny all party differences on this question. But it had been the Conservative-dominated National Government which had passed the Government of India Act in 1935, which had clearly envisaged a transition to dominion status. Churchill's stance should not be taken as typical of the Conservative Party as a whole. According to Anthony Eden, Churchill's 'laments on India and Burma' did the Tories no good at all (quoted in Dutton, 1996, p. 320). Philip Noel-Baker, Labour's Commonwealth Secretary, recalled that it was Eden's job 'to keep Churchill away from the House while the Bill went through because if he came into the Chamber he might be unable to stop himself speaking against' (Lapping, 1985, p. 87). When Labour's bill came up for its second reading on 10 July 1947, Churchill was not in the Commons and the Opposition's objections were presented in moderate terms by Harold Macmillan.

As far as the rest of the Empire was concerned, Labour made significant moves in the field of colonial development, particularly in Nigeria and the Gold Coast, but there was no headlong rush towards independence. Britain would remain an imperial power into the foreseeable future. Back in 1943 Attlee had argued for the maintenance of 'the British Commonwealth as an international entity' so as to enable Britain to 'carry our full weight in the post-war world with the US and USSR' (Porter, 1994, pp. 256–7). Hugh Dalton once described the colonies as 'pullulating, poverty-stricken, diseased nigger communities' (Morgan, 1984, p. 194). Owing to a shortage of investment capital, concludes Henry Pelling, the Labour government 'could do little for the colonial empire except to indicate its willingness to see a progressive expansion of constitutional development at the local level' (Pelling, 1984, p. 267).

In Malaya, Labour embarked upon a military confrontation to root out Communist infiltration, a process which would continue throughout the 1950s. What is striking, however, is the degree to which the whole colonial question transcended party divisions. In 1945 George Hall, Labour's Colonial Secretary, thanked his Conservative predecessor for laying the foundations of his own policy, and such bipartisan sentiments were to be reiterated by Oliver Lyttelton in the Conservative government of 1951.

Bevin and the Labour government as a whole adopted an extremely cool attitude towards the first signs of a European federalist movement in the late 1940s. Not that Bevin was as unsympathetic to all ideas of European integration as was once thought. During his first three years in office he explored several proposals for closer cooperation including a customs union. These might have made more progress but for the inherent caution of the Treasury and the Board of Trade. Thereafter, however, Bevin became increasingly hostile to the growing view on the continent that integration should proceed along supranational lines (Greenwood, 1992, pp. 7–29). In any case, Bevin's primary interest lay in securing adequate defence arrangements. This meant committing the United States to defend the European continent, and he was far more interested in developing Britain's links with the United States than in fostering European co-operation. With its shattered economy Europe at this time scarcely looked like an inviting partner for the British government, and when in 1950 the Schuman Plan proposed a pooling of sovereignty over the coal and steel industries of western Europe, Labour held aloof. With Churchill and other leading Conservatives such as Macmillan and David Maxwell Fyfe apparently enthusiastic supporters of closer European integration, this did seem to be an area where the consensus did not run. Later events, however, would show that a Conservative government was no more interested than Labour in the development of a united Europe, if this involved a loss of sovereignty.

If the establishment of a post-war consensus is viewed as a movement by the two leading parties towards a common centre ground, that process was clearly not complete by 1945 in the case of the Conservatives. Indeed, in so far as there existed a core of policies common to the two parties by the end of the war, the electorate clearly did not fully believe in the Conservatives' commitment to it. Historians who have questioned the extent to which the war itself created a two-party consensus point to the importance of the immediate post-war years for the development of Conservative thinking. According to Kevin Jefferys, for example, 'the profound shock of Labour's overwhelming victory was . . . to be of greater importance than the experience of war in shifting the Conservative party towards a fundamental reassessment of its domestic policy' (Jefferys, 1987b, p. 144; Eatwell, 1979, p. 159). Kenneth Morgan points to the revival of the Conservative Research Department at the end of 1945 as an admission that the party's disastrous performance at the recent election resulted from its having no credible stance towards questions of social reconstruction (Morgan, p. 1990, p. 32). Similarly Samuel Beer asserts that by 1945 Conservatism had not made a full or definite commitment to either the welfare state or the managed economy (Beer, 1965, p. 308).

If for no other reason than Labour's electoral success in 1945, the Conservatives had no alternative but to integrate some of Labour's thinking into their own programme more clearly than they had yet managed to do. As Butler put it, 'until the progressive features of our thought had been fully exposed to public view, no one was going to kill Attlee in order to make Churchill king' (Butler, 1971, p. 132). Quintin Hogg thought the time was ripe for promulgating a new Tamworth Manifesto. This would necessitate asserting the ascendancy of the younger progressive elements in the party over the traditional libertarian strain. It was unlikely that the septuagenarian Churchill would play a major role in this process and in fact it was only the insistence of the 1946 party conference for a clear statement of what the party stood for that overrode his reluctance to authorize work on policy re-examination. Fortunately, as Leader of the Opposition, Churchill operated as little more than a part-time politician and largely limited himself to making speeches on matters of foreign and defence policy. Significantly, we find Eden, who in many ways acted as the unofficial day-to-day Leader of the Opposition at this time, criticizing a policy draft presented to him in the spring of 1946 which spoke in terms of balanced budgets, repayment of international debts and a reliance on market forces to create employment. According to Eden, it was not enough 'just to say we believe in freedom and free enterprise. What is our conception of the state in relation to industry?' (Ramsden, 1995, pp. 141–2).

Furthermore, one of the beneficial effects of electoral defeat in 1945 and the loss of 173 seats was to clear out a large amount of parliamentary dead wood at a single stroke. 'Almost without exception', noted one progressive Tory, 'we are well rid of them all. So, the field is clear and we can start building a leadership and a party for the next twenty years' (quoted in Ramsden, 1995, p. 93). About half of all Conservative MPs returned at the election had no previous parliamentary experience and the average age of the parliamentary party in 1945 was only 41. The fact that 41 Conservative MPs – a fifth of the parliamentary party – signed the Tory Reform Committee manifesto, *Forward – by the Right* in October 1945 gives some indication of the outlook of the new intake (Ball, 1995, p. 111). Then the election of 1950 saw the recruitment of a large number of talented MPs who would set the tone of Conservatism in the 1950s and 1960s. The formation that year of the 'One Nation' group of younger MPs interested in progressive social legislation was symbolic of the change.

The leading figure in the reformulation of Conservative thinking was R. A. Butler, aided by the bright young men who, under his direction, staffed the revitalized Conservative Research Department, which became a think-tank of new ideas. From this fertile source there flowed a stream of new policy initiatives, which gradually transformed the party's tarnished image, enabling it to recapture much of the centre ground in the ongoing battle of ideas. In an important speech in March 1946 Butler called for a total reorganization of the social structure on which the party rested, an acceptance of redistributive taxation and a repudiation of *laissez-faire* economics. The *Manchester Guardian* commented that such goals would have the support of the majority of the Parliamentary Labour Party, while from the Conservative right Brendan Bracken wrote scathingly of 'neo-Socialists' who favoured nationalizing railways, electricity, gas and many other things (Horne, 1988, p. 299).

The publication of the *Industrial Charter* in 1947 was perhaps the nearest thing to the new Tamworth Manifesto for which Hogg had called. Butler saw the need to counter the charge that Conservatives were the party of industrial free-for-all. The Charter was therefore first and foremost an assurance that modern Conservatism would maintain a strong central guidance over the management of the economy in the interests of efficiency and full employment (R. A. Butler, 1971, p. 146). It accepted the nationalization of the mines, railways and Bank of England and spoke of new machinery for economic planning and fixing wages. But more important than the Charter's details – many of which were in fact dropped when the Tories returned to power – was the general impression which it gave that the Conservatives were moving towards the centre ground of benevolent interventionism already occupied by Labour. As John Ramsden has argued, its primary importance was political rather than industrial or economic (Ramsden, 1980, p. 111). What had seemed beyond the pale of Conservative politics only a decade earlier, when Macmillan had written *The Middle Way*, now occupied the mainstream of the party's thought. It was, he recalled, a source of great satisfaction to him. 'For the leaders of my party and its members as a whole had now broadly accepted the policies for which I had so vainly striven in the past' (Macmillan, 1969, p. 312). The *Manchester Guardian* even wrote of 'Tory Socialism'. The Charter was accepted by the party conference in 1947 when Eden, reminding the delegates of their tradition of social reform, declared that Conservatives were not a 'party of unbridled, brutal capitalism'. The handful of critics on the Right were easily defeated. It was followed in 1948 by the less important *Agricultural Charter* which basically accepted the interventionism of the government's Agriculture Act of 1947 with guaranteed price support for farmers.

The Tory manifesto of 1950 was based on the Research Department's *The Right Road for Britain*, which had been published in July 1949. Entitled *This is the Road*, the manifesto seemed to differ from Labour's only in so far as it still stressed the importance of personal initiative and promised to return road transport and steel to the private sector. According to Peter Hennessy it was 'of long-term significance . . . because it endorsed implicitly the Attleean settlement . . . The Keynesian and Beveridgite essentials would be intact whatever the outcome' (Hennessy, 1992, p. 388). The Tories insisted that they regarded 'the maintenance of full employment as the first aim of a Conservative Government'. Butler and the Research Department had thus completed the transformation of the Conservative Party from its pre-war stance to one that was both interventionist and forward-looking.

The Labour Party went into the General Election of 1950 with a new and somewhat random shopping list of industries to be nationalized, but one which would only have brought a further 500,000 workers into the public sector. Morrison had been careful to stress the empirical nature of the new programme at the party conference that year, and, as Labour's chief electoral strategist, sought to commit the party to a policy based on consolidation rather than innovation in order to retain the middle-class vote which Labour had been so successful in winning in 1945. In terms of the balance between the public and private sectors, Labour seemed to have reached something of a plateau. Further significant shifts might take place at some unspecified time in the future, but for the time being it seemed that the party's leaders believed that the mixture was about right. In fact little was made of the party's nationalization plans in the campaign itself. The Tories too, committed now to the welfare state and the mixed economy, presented themselves as a party of moderation, while trying to portray their opponents as class warriors. The Conservative campaign emphasized that the welfare system and full employment would be as safe with them as with Labour. 'We pledge ourselves to maintain and improve the Health Service', the manifesto insisted. Their message was not that they would dismantle the post-war settlement, but that they would manage it more efficiently. As the *Manchester Guardian* remarked, the Conservatives had 'never in their history produced so enlightened a statement on social policy – from full employment to education and the social services'. The practical effect, therefore, was that the party battalions fought their battles over a remarkably narrow field of conflict. Moderation seemed to be the order of the day. The rhetoric of confrontational politics was maintained. Churchill spoke of a 'momentous choice' between 'individual liberty and state domination', while Tory slogans stressed freedom, consumer choice and economic opportunity, but this was scarcely a reflection of opposing policies. Harold Macmillan noted the way in which both parties had tended to move towards the middle ground. All but a few of the extreme left of the Labour Party were beaten; only three Communist candidates retained their deposits (Horne, 1988, p. 318).

Labour survived the election but with its massive overall majority of 1945 now reduced to a mere five seats. The closeness of the result, presaging an early return to the polls, and the feeling that Labour had lost its mandate, rather than any fundamental policy differences, made the new Parliament tense and acrimonious. But there were few further advances along the paths of socialism. Labour's shopping list of industries was quietly dropped; the *Daily Express* described Gaitskell's 1951 budget as a truly Tory measure.

Beset by death, illness and resignation among his senior ministers, Attlee went to the country again in October 1951. The party's manifesto was even more moderate than in 1950. It did not even contain the word socialism. There was no shopping list for nationalization, but only a vague promise to take into public ownership certain unspecified industries which were 'failing the nation'. The two major parties were increasingly trying to appeal to the same interests and emotions in the electorate. Of course, politicians did their best to emphasize points of party difference by exaggerating the position of their opponents. For Labour, Michael Foot warned against 'the mass unemployment which we always have under the Tories', while the Labour candidate for Bridgewater predicted that a Conservative government would mean wars all over the globe. Even Morrison accused Churchill of being a warmonger, a cry that was taken up in menacing tones by the *Daily Mirror*. But after six years of Labour government, much of it characterized by Crippsian austerity, the country was ready for a change. With an overall majority of 17 seats (though Labour still held the advantage in terms of the popular vote), the Conservatives with Churchill at their head returned to power. The reality of the consensus would now be put to the test.

3

The Consensus Confirmed, 1951–70

Labour built its 1951 election campaign around the fear that a Conservative victory would result in divisive domestic policies and aggressive and dangerous policies abroad. There were predictions of the dismantling of the welfare state, conflict with the trade unions, renewed militarism and an end to colonial development. In fact none of these predictions was borne out by events. One factor was the narrowness of the Conservative victory. *The Times* argued that the Conservatives would be honour bound to see themselves as a national rather than a party government. Even had they been so inclined, no one believed the Tories had a mandate to undo Labour's post-war legacy (Porter, 1994, p. 281). The historian of Churchill's post-war administration concludes that 'one of the most remarkable features of the Government was the extent that Conservative policy followed on logically from Labour policy in the preceding six years' (Seldon, 1981, p. 421). In his first parliamentary speech on returning to the premiership Churchill announced prophetically: 'Controversy there must be on some of the issues before us, but this will be a small part of the work and interests we have in common.' After they had been consolidated in power with an increased majority by the 1955 election, Attlee told the Durham Miners' Gala that the Conservatives owed their victory to their appropriation of Labour's policies: 'They have had to accept what we have done – many things which 20, 30 or 40 years ago they would have denounced as heresies and silly socialism' (K. Harris, 1982, p. 534). A year later Attlee's successor explained to a foreign visitor that, though there were still some differences between the two parties, these were far smaller than before 1939 and that 'to a large extent the Conservatives had taken over the policies of the post-war Labour Government' (Williams, 1983, p. 485). The consensus in fact was confirmed.

An important factor was the type of Conservative who now dominated the party. The government, of course, was headed by Winston Churchill, anxious to rid the party of its 1930s image. But at seventy-seven years of age the prime minister did little more than set the framework as far as domestic politics were concerned, reserving his failing energies for foreign and defence matters. The dominant voices of the new Conservatism throughout the 1950s were those of R. A. Butler, Harold Macmillan and, notwithstanding his immersion in questions of diplomacy, Anthony Eden. Despite the sometimes bitter personal rivalries between these three men, in terms of political philosophy there was little to separate them. Butler, of course, had already done much during the war and after to establish his credentials as a consensus politician on the left of the party. Macmillan had been deeply affected by pre-war unemployment in his constituency of Stockton-on-Tees. An early convert to Keynesianism before that economic philosophy had gained widespread acceptance, he never permitted his colleagues to forget their commitment to full employment. On becoming Conservative leader in 1957 Macmillan pronounced, in the best tradition of Disraeli's 'One Nation', that 'we have never been, and I trust that while I am your leader, we never will be, a party of any class or sectional interest' (Horne, 1989, p. 17). His farewell message read out to the 1963 party conference carried the same essential sentiment. 'I have seen our policies develop into that pragmatic and sensible compromise between the extremes of collectivism and individualism for which the party has always stood in its great periods' (Ramsden, 1996, p. 1). Eden's biographer has written: 'I always found his brand of humane, liberal and progressive Conservatism, born in the trenches on the Western Front in 1916, the only version that appealed to me' (James, 1986,

p. xi). Indeed, during the war Eden had toyed with the idea of forming a new centrist coalition headed by Ernest Bevin and himself, or trying to construct a progressive Tory party with the help of younger men such as Butler.

Churchill, anxious to preserve domestic peace to pave the way for a last effort on his part to pull the world back from the brink of thermonuclear disaster, ensured that men such as these would set the tone of his government. 'It was a Government of Tory wets, for whom social harmony was a higher priority than economic efficiency' (Addison, 1992, p. 387). The momentum of events since 1945 and the ongoing aspirations of the British people probably left Churchill little room for manoeuvre. His wooing of the Liberal Party with the offer of a cabinet post to its leader, Clement Davies, was a further sign of the prime minister's determination to form a moderate and broadly-based government (Addison, 1992, p. 408).

Churchill appointed Butler (rather than Oliver Lyttelton, as many had predicted) to the Exchequer. Back in 1947 Lyttelton, whose instincts were with the primacy of the market, had warned Churchill of the need to reverse Labour's strategy through a policy of decontrol and a floating pound. Eden returned, almost inevitably, to the Foreign Office, universally recognized as heir-in-waiting for the premiership; and Macmillan went to the Ministry of Housing, a post which assumed political prominence in view of the party's commitment to build 300,000 houses in a single year. There his programme was, as *The Economist* commented in 1953, 'of the kind that might typically be expected from a Coalition government'. Another important appointment was that of the emollient Walter Monckton as Minister of Labour. Maxwell Fyfe, whom many had expected to get the job, had ruffled feathers by hinting at the possibility of trade union legislation from a future Conservative government, obliging Churchill to intervene during the election campaign to insist that no such legislation would be introduced in the next parliament. Notable right-wing figures such as Ralph Assheton and Charles Waterhouse were excluded from office. From Labour's benches Richard Crossman, recognizing that 'the real free enterprisers and deflationists seem to have been left out', judged that the new Conservative cabinet was 'only very slightly to the right of the most recent Attlee Cabinet'. Just as Attlee had run 'what was virtually a coalition policy on a party basis, so Churchill may well do the same' (Crossman, 1981, p. 30).

The new government's economic policy was central to its overall strategy and a critical element in the consolidation of the consensus. Lord Croham, a future Head of the Treasury, believed that there was less change in 1951 than between any two governments in the whole post-war era (Hennessy and Seldon, 1987, p. 79). Certainly, the new government stopped short of restoring the full-bloodied capitalist economy which critics had anticipated and which would have pleased some backbench Tories such as Ralph Assheton, the powerful chairman of the party's Finance Committee. In fact it almost immediately introduced an Excess Profits Tax. A Treasury plan, code-named 'Robot', which would have allowed the pound to float and involved abandoning the commitment to full employment, was put forward in the spring of 1952, but such free-market adventures were quickly abandoned. The idea behind 'Robot' was to take the pressure off the external balance of payments and put it on the internal economy. A falling pound would then bring imports and exports back into equilibrium. Eden took much credit for killing off the plan which he attacked on social grounds, particularly the serious impact it would have on unemployment. Any other policy, he insisted, including a sharp cut in the rearmament programme was to be preferred (Dutton, 1996, p. 267). The rejection of 'Robot' was clearly a seminal moment in the confirmation of the post-war consensus.

Fears that Churchill's government would preside over a return to the mass unemployment of the 1930s therefore proved unfounded. When it did threaten to rise in 1952 the government prepared some highly interventionist schemes of public works to hold it down. Churchill himself advocated the reclamation of marginal land, highway development and the construction of a barrage across the River Severn (Gilbert, 1988, p. 734). In 1955 the monthly average of registered unemployed dropped to 232,000, little more than one per cent of the workforce. Calls to 'set the people free' proved to be little more than rhetoric, while the government even recognized the need to continue the rationing of basic foods for the time being. Eventually they were able to continue the trend begun by Harold Wilson with his 'bonfire of controls' in 1948.

Early in 1954 *The Economist* invented the mythical composite personality of Mr Butskell, a combination of the names of Butler and his Labour predecessor, Hugh Gaitskell (*The Economist*, 13 February 1954). Ever since, the hybrid concept of Butskellism has epitomized the consensus, particularly in its economic aspects. The economist Samuel Brittan has described it as 'an interesting mixture of planning and freedom, based on the economic teachings of Lord Keynes' (Brittan, 1964, p. 162). Yet some historians have disputed the extent of continuity between Gaitskell and Butler. Keith Middlemas, for example, points to the revival of interest in monetary policy and the reduction of planning under Butler (Middlemas, 1986, p. 269). Neil Rollings insists that Labour politicians remained more committed, even in the mid-1950s, to the idea of direct controls than has often been suggested (Rollings, 1994, p. 192). Gaitskell, as his biographer shows, objected to the term 'Butskellism' as a 'silly catchword', and claimed that he was much more willing than Butler to use the budget as an instrument of economic control. Certainly the two men had different long-term visions of the distribution of wealth (Williams, 1979, p. 313).

But such criticisms are a counsel of perfection in the analysis of a fundamental consensus. The general pattern remained a basic commitment to the mixed economy and Keynesian budgetary planning and demand management. Butler was anxious to show that the Conservatives were not the party of unemployment, and resisted calls from some of his colleagues for drastic cuts in public expenditure. Though Gaitskell may not have felt flattered to be so closely linked with a Conservative, contemporaries cannot have been entirely mistaken in their perceptions. It is worth noting the reported reaction of the Conservative MP, Robert Boothby, to Butler's appointment in October 1951. More than two years before *The Economist* coined the phrase 'Butskellism', he is said to have remarked, 'Why that's Gaitskell all over again, but from Cambridge' (Crossman, 1981, p. 30). Butler himself conceded that he and Gaitskell both spoke the language of Keynesianism, albeit 'with different accents and with a differing emphasis' (R. A. Butler, 1971, p. 160). Gaitskell's own reaction to the first manifestations of Tory government is also instructive. 'As to their policy', he wrote, 'they have really done exactly what we would have done, and have followed the same lines on controls, economic planning etc.' (Williams, 1983, p. 307). Importantly, after a difficult beginning as a result of the Korean War, Butler's stewardship proved reasonably successful. It was a time when world factors were more generally favourable to the British economy than in any subsequent period. Butler's years as chancellor thus came to be seen as a model for future practice by governments of both political complexions.

The new government's attitude towards its inheritance of state-owned industry provided an important test of the reality of the consensus. Experience proved that nationalization was an element of the consensus where rhetoric and practice were widely separated. Churchill's government confirmed those boundaries between the public and private sectors which survived largely intact for the next three decades. The Conservatives denationalized only the steel and road haulage industries. In the case of steel, Labour's plans had not yet progressed very far, nationalization only having come into effect in January 1951, so the process of denationalization was relatively straightforward. In any case the government preserved a large measure of central control through the Iron and Steel Board, despite the preference of some ministers such as Harry Crookshank and Lord Woolton for a more radical approach. As John Ramsden has put it, 'considering that steel was intended to mark the great divide between the parties, both the policy and the way in which it was defended fell well short of a ringing endorsement of capitalism' (Ramsden, 1995, p. 251). The Conservative bill caused little controversy, though Labour went through the ritual of opposition. At one time debate was adjourned as less than 40 MPs were present (Seldon, 1981, p. 191). The Transport Bill proved more contentious, but in the end road haulage was only partially returned to the private sector because of the difficulty of finding buyers. Denationalization went no further. Churchill stressed: 'It is only where we believed that a measure of nationalisation was a real hindrance to our island life that we have reversed the policy' (quoted in Seldon, 1981, p. 187). Nationalization had almost been stripped of its ideological content. As a Labour policy document of 1952 did not repeat an earlier threat to nationalize the chemical and sugar industries, it seemed that a new status quo had been established in this once controversial field.

In the elections of 1950 and 1951 Labour had predicted that a Conservative victory would mean drastic cutbacks in the social services. Harriet Jones maintains that underneath a 'veneer of consensual politics there lay deep differences between party attitudes towards the state provision of social benefits'. Even the 'One Nation' Group ruled out 'equality' as a goal of Conservative social policy. She beleives that Conservative ministers intent on a change of direction found their room for manoeuvre extremely limited and writes of a 'consensus born of constraint' (Gorst, Johnman and Lucas, 1991, pp. 33–4). Be that as it may, Jones concedes that in practice the 'political transfer of power. . . did not seem to have much effect on social policy' (Gorst, *et al.*, 1991, p. 38). In his first budget Butler did introduce some health service charges, but Gaitskell himself had been the first chancellor to breach the principle of a health service free at the point of delivery in his budget of 1951. Thereafter, however, as the economy strengthened, the Conservatives actually increased spending on the social services, taking satisfaction in proclaiming their virtue in this respect. The cost of the social services, as a proportion of total government spending, rose from 39.2 per cent in 1951 to 43 per cent in 1955 (Addison, 1992, p. 419). Consolidated current and capital expenditure on the National Health Service almost doubled between 1951 and 1962 (Coopey, Fielding and Tiratsoo, 1993, p. 13). The broad fabric of the welfare state was thus maintained, even enhanced. In December 1951 the Cabinet's Economy Committee dropped plans for hospital charges. It was a sign that attacks on the welfare state were politically unacceptable. Successive Conservative ministers of health in the 1950s buried the notion that the Tories were out to destroy the National Health Service. By the end of the decade it had become 'almost a part of the Constitution' (Hennessy, 1992, p. 122). A particularly important hospital building programme was initiated in the early 1960s. The Guillebaud Committee reported in 1956 that the health service was providing value for money and the government accepted its conclusions. 'It is difficult to imagine', concludes Anthony Seldon, 'that Labour would have managed the N.H.S. very differently in these years' (Seldon, 1981, p. 270).

It is, of course, the Labour Party with which the trade union movement traditionally enjoys a close and intimate relationship, yet during Churchill's government the unions were brought closer to a Conservative administration than for many years past. Churchill, with his role during the General Strike not forgotten, was keen to pursue a policy of industrial appeasement, even if this meant inflationary wage settlements. He was determined, wrote Woolton, that there should be few industrial strikes during his period as prime minister (Woolton, 1959, pp. 379–80). Sir Walter Monckton, the new Minister of Labour, was predisposed towards conciliation and all his energies were devoted to bringing the two sides of industry together. Monckton's typical reaction to an industrial dispute was to set up an inquiry to enforce a compromise. At the last moment, however, under instructions from the prime minister, he was always ready to give the unions what they demanded rather than weaken the corporate structure that had been created during and after the war. The price of harmony was therefore usually paid in terms of an inflationary pay award, while Monckton's emollient tactics earned him the nickname of the 'oil-can' – though one perceptive observer described him as 'the architect of slippery slopes' (Colville, 1981, p. 183). It was an astonishing commentary on this period that Arthur Deakin, General Secretary of the Transport and General Workers' Union, could say in 1953, 'I believe Sir Walter Monckton has given us a square deal and we have been able to do things that were difficult to do under our own people' (quoted in Seldon, 1981, p. 202). Not until the London bus strike of 1958 did an industrial dispute become a matter of serious conflict between government and opposition. One commentator has written of the 'industrial Butskellism' of these years (Davis Smith, 1990, p. 142).

Anthony Seldon has shown that across the range of domestic ministries, from fuel and power to pensions via agriculture, the degree of genuine inter-party disagreement was kept to a minimum and the consensus maintained. Housing was probably the aspect of social policy which most divided the parties and the Rent Act of 1957, which lifted control over rents on 400,000 houses, was one of the few legislative measures of the 1950s which exposed a clear difference of purpose and ideology between government and opposition. The Conservatives defended the rights of private property and expressed a faith in the market as the most efficient means of satisfying normal housing needs. Labour, by contrast, favoured public provision and wanted to protect tenants from exploitation in private rented accommodation (Lowe, 1990b, p. 31). This, however, was an exception. As much as anything else, Tories were determined to liberate themselves from their image of the 1930s. 'The important thing in the 1950s', argues John Biffen, 'was to live down the bad, black days of interwar Britain' (Biffen, 1988, p. 16). Though Labour made education policy an area of vigorous debate, *The Times* could still comment in April 1953 that there was little to divide the two parties. Debate was beginning on the value of comprehensive schools, but this had not yet become a serious issue of inter-party dispute.

Much the same picture emerges from an examination of the government's overseas policy. None of the Labour Party's dire predictions proved correct, at least until the Suez disaster of 1956. Labour backbenchers, particularly those on the left, found plenty to criticize, but as far as the party leadership was concerned, disagreements were rare and 'mainly on questions of priorities' (Seldon, 1981, p. 415). Eden could justly tell the party conference in 1954: 'I always believe that the more bipartisan our foreign policy can be, the stronger the authority of the Foreign Secretary of the day' (quoted in Seldon, 1981, p. 414). Far from intensifying the cold war, Churchill laboured mightily, if vainly, to bring the great powers together at a summit conference. More fruitfully, Eden as Foreign Secretary achieved a string of diplomatic triumphs, not least his skilful handling of the Geneva conference on Indochina in 1954. The Conservatives, of course, had no difficulty in seeking to maintain the basis of Labour's foreign policy – a close partnership with the United States in a still tense and dangerous world.

Churchill and Eden believed that the Special Relationship had been weakened during the years of Labour government but in practice found it no easier than their predecessors to place Britain's dealings with the United States upon that basis of equality which they held to be their country's due (Dutton, 1996, p. 353). In the first defence debate in the Commons after the 1951 election, Churchill paid tribute to the outgoing Labour government 'for several most important decisions about our defence policy which . . . form the foundation on which we stand today' (quoted in Seldon, 1981, p. 15). Critically, the Conservatives continued Labour's policy of giving priority to the RAF and building up a nuclear bomber force as the basis of the country's front-line defence.

The foreign policy consensus appeared to break down in a most spectacular fashion in 1956, after Eden had succeeded to the premiership. The occasion was the famous Suez Crisis when Britain, in conjunction with France and in collusion with Israel, invaded Egypt in response to Colonel Nasser's nationalization of the Suez Canal Company. The government's actions were roundly condemned by the overwhelming majority of world opinion and there was no doubting the sincerity of the vehement opposition coming from the Labour Party. For many the normal courtesies of cross-party behaviour became for a while impossible. Yet it is important to stress that Labour's fury was directed at the way in which Eden tried to recover the canal rather than the government's underlying case. In its initial reaction Labour had been at one with the Conservatives in condemning Nasser's action. Gaitskell described it as 'high-handed and totally unjustified', while another Labour MP, Reginald Paget, spoke of the perils of appeasing dictators (James, 1986, pp. 455–6). Labour's last Foreign Secretary, Herbert Morrison, urged the government not to be 'too nervous'. He favoured acting through the United Nations, but only if that body was expeditious and effective. Otherwise it would be the duty of MPs such as himself to support the government in the use of force. It was the government's well-concealed resort to force, at a time when many still hoped for a peaceful settlement through the United Nations, together with the first hints of collusion with Israel, which fractured the bipartisan response to Nasser's aggression.

Policy towards Europe provides one of the most interesting, and even surprising, illustrations of the consensus. By his stirring speeches in the late 1940s Churchill had put himself at the head of the movement for a more united Europe, and enthusiasts expected great things from him when the Conservatives returned to power after the cool response of the Labour government. But Churchill's rhetoric had not been analysed as closely as it should have been. Indeed, soon after his return to government Churchill insisted that he had 'never thought that Britain or the British Commonwealth should, either individually or collectively, become an integral part of a European Federation and had never given the slightest support to the idea' (quoted in Dutton, 1996, p. 292). Pro-Europeans in the cabinet, such as Macmillan and Maxwell Fyfe, found their high hopes quickly dashed by Churchill and Eden. At a press conference shortly after taking office, Eden made it perfectly clear that the new government had no more intention of joining the European Defence Community than had its predecessor. At Columbia University in January 1952 he declared that the idea of Britain joining a European federation was 'something which we know, in our bones, we cannot do' (Dutton, 1996, p. 297). Thus the pattern was set which would see the countries of western Europe, with Britain excluded, move towards the creation of the Common Market with the signing of the Treaty of Rome in 1957.

Commonwealth and colonial policy showed how far the Conservative Party of the 1950s had moved from its pre-war traditions. There were still right-wing imperialists holding high office – Lord Salisbury even became Commonwealth Secretary in 1952 – but it was not they who set the tone of the government's policy. Even Churchill, himself a product of the age of Victorian imperialism, bowed to the inevitable. The inexorable progress of the colonial territories towards independence was not really a contentious issue in these years, however much Labour tried to make it such. The Opposition's fury was largely a sham. Kavanagh and Morris conclude that it was in the area of colonial policy 'that post-war bipartisanship was perhaps at its strongest' (Kavanagh and Morris, 1989, p. 97). Oliver Lyttelton, appointed Colonial Secretary in 1951, was the first of a series of liberal-minded ministers, culminating with Iain Macleod in 1959, who oversaw the process by which the old Empire was transformed into a multiracial Commonwealth. By Macleod's time the rush towards decolonization was becoming almost a stampede, with the government now willing to concede independence well in advance of being forced to do so.

By the mid-1950s, therefore, the consensus had become a centre-piece of British political life. Writing in 1955, Robert McKenzie described the way in which the parties still conducted 'furious arguments about the comparatively minor issues that separate them' (McKenzie, 1955, p. 586). A Labour MP of these years later recalled that there had seemed 'every prospect of Britain proceeding indefinitely on a Social Democratic course . . . Hence it would not matter greatly whether the Labour or Conservative Party won general elections' (Wyatt, 1977, p. 42). It was perhaps no coincidence that in 1953 Edward Hyams wrote a novel entitled *Gentian Violet* in which the leading character succeeded in getting elected to Parliament both as a Conservative and as a socialist without being found out. The General Election of 1955, noted David Butler, must have been the first since the Labour Party achieved full maturity 'in which its supporters did not believe that their victory was essential to save the country from unemployment, war and misery' (D. Butler, 1955, p. 94). Hugh Dalton described it as the 'most tedious, apathetic, uninteresting' in which he had fought (Pimlott, 1986b, p. 671). In his personal statement to the electorate Anthony Eden reaffirmed the Conservatives' commitment to the post-war settlement in language which showed how far his party had moved to the centre ground. 'We have seen both employment and earnings reach new high levels', he declared. 'We have seen new houses and new schools and new factories built and building, and soon we shall see new hospitals, too. We have seen the social services extended and improved' (quoted in Shepherd, 1994, p. 100).

After another Conservative victory, Parliament reassembled to debate the Queen's Speech of a government now headed by Eden. After Attlee had spoken, the prime minister could 'only thank him' for his words. His speech 'was so kind and so gentle and so generally approving that I feel we can go forward with the execution of this formidable programme under the benevolent aegis of the Honourable Members opposite' (quoted in K. Harris, 1982, p. 536). Across a wide range of policies the Conservatives had pursued and continued to pursue a broad line of continuity from their Labour predecessors. There had been few sharp reversals. Indeed, the Tories had tended to accelerate trends already marked out by Labour. The era of change and reorganization inaugurated by the war-time coalition was at an end and the Conservatives had no intention of reversing what had been accomplished since 1940. There had been no second watershed despite the change of government in 1951. According to Paul Addison, 'in their different ways the two main parties [now] lacked ideological purpose' (Addison, 1985, p. 198). In 1960 Daniel Bell published *The End of Ideology*. Its subtitle, *On the Exhaustion of Political Ideas in the Fifties*, was revealing. Bell argued that an intellectual consensus now existed on such issues as the welfare state, the mixed economy and political pluralism. 'In that sense', he concluded, 'the ideological age has ended' (Bell, 1960, p. 373).

Not all Conservatives were happy that the arrival of a Conservative government had seemed to make so little difference to the way the country was run. All the rhetoric about liberating the economy from Labour's trammels had not, after all, amounted to very much in practice. The strain of economic liberalism within the Tory ranks was never completely submerged. Ralph Assheton, as party chairman, had drawn upon the writings of the free-market economist, Friedrich von Hayek, to argue the case against government interventionism even before the end of the war. Thereafter, a right-wing minority had maintained an unswerving opposition to the changes introduced by Attlee's government and called for a full-blooded revival of free enterprise. Enoch Powell, elected to Parliament for the first time in 1950, criticized Chancellor Butler's first statement to the Commons in 1952 precisely because of 'its similarity in kind to those in 1947 and 1949' and because it contrasted with 'the expansionist and libertarian spirit in which the government entered upon office' (Cosgrave, 1989, p. 126). In 1954 even the One Nation Group called for a policy of denationalization.

The Conservative cabinet minister, Iain Macleod – 'the Essential Post-War Tory, the Welfare State Tory, the Tory New Dealer' – was an object of particular scorn for the Right (Shepherd, 1994, p. 150). For the most part, however, the party's individualists and free marketeers recognized that they were a beleaguered minority running against an irresistible tide of collectivism. Anthony Fisher, a young RAF pilot attracted by the free market philosophy, was advised that an entry into politics would be a waste of time and effort (Muller, 1996, p. 90). Fisher went on to help found the right-wing Institute of Economic Affairs in 1955. But for the time being such think-tanks made almost no impression upon contemporary political debate.

For Labour these years were marked, as so often when the party is out of power, by division and internecine strife. The beginnings of a left-wing revolt against the leadership had been seen while Labour was still in power, when Bevan, Wilson and John Freeman resigned from the government after Gaitskell introduced charges for false teeth and spectacles in 1951. Frustrated ambition on Bevan's part was also an important factor. During the 1950s the left had its moments of triumph. In Parliament it often took the lead, since the party hierarchy found little in the Conservatives' policies to which it took serious exception. 'The vacuum of opposition was therefore filled by left-wing noise' (Sked and Cook, 1979, p. 136). In particular, the Bevanites rejected Attlee's continuing bipartisanship and clamoured for an alternative, socialist foreign policy. At the 1952 party conference the left all but swept the board in the constituency party section of elections to the National Executive Committee. In 1953 Labour adopted a policy document, 'Challenge to Britain', which promised a further dose of nationalization. It also promised an extension of comprehensive education and the phasing out of all private schools, together with the abolition of health service charges. In the main, however, the right wing kept its hands firmly on the reins of power.

The critical development was the leadership battle which ensued when Attlee finally decided to retire after the General Election of 1955. Gaitskell's comprehensive victory over Morrison and Bevan ensured that, perhaps more clearly than at any time in its previous history, Labour would compete with the Tories for the centre ground of British politics. For Gaitskell was far less concerned than Attlee had been to use the leadership to unite the disparate factions that make up the British Labour Party. He never sought to conceal his own position on the party's intellectual right or his contempt for its Marxist fringe. As one left-wing critic bemoaned, the Gaitskellites 'saw Labour achieving power and retaining it only through a more efficient, technological management of a capitalist society' (Duff, 1971, p. 77). Of equal importance was the clear ascendancy of the revisionist right in the intellectual battles of the 1950s. While the left seemed bankrupt of new ideas, the right produced an impressive flow of fresh thinking. Of seminal importance was Anthony Crosland's *The Future of Socialism*, published in 1956. Crosland argued that socialism was about equality rather than public ownership. If that was true, nationalization could be relegated to the status of a redundant instrument in the achievement of a socialist state. Keynesian economics would be sufficient to secure Labour's aims. Crosland's message showed that gulfs did remain between the two main parties – particularly in terms of long-term goals. At the same time he conceded that the main debates over economic policy had now been concluded, that affluence was guaranteed and that mass unemployment had probably been eliminated for all time. Labour's 1957 policy document, *Industry and Society*, suggested that old-style nationalization had been replaced in the party's thinking by new ideas such as buying up equity shares in industrial firms. By the end of the decade, concludes Kenneth Morgan, 'the general trend appeared to be a drift away from anything that could reasonably be called socialism' (Morgan, 1990, p. 183). The year 1960 saw the setting up of the Campaign for Democratic Socialism. The inclusion of the word 'socialism' in its title was perhaps misleading since its aims were to disseminate the revisionist ideas of Crosland and Gaitskell and to advance the supporters of such ideas to positions of power within the party.

Gaitskell did have plenty of trouble from Labour's left particularly after the party's third successive electoral defeat in 1959. His battles to remove Clause IV from the party's constitution – 'we have

. . . long ago come to accept . . . a mixed economy' – and to stave off a conference commitment to unilateral nuclear disarmament, gave advance warning of the growing power of the left that would one day confront his successor. But the party bequeathed to Harold Wilson's leadership following Gaitskell's premature death in 1963 was firmly anchored in the centre ground of British politics, notwithstanding Wilson's earlier dalliance on the Bevanite left. Labour was a realistic contender for power once more.

The Conservatives were in power for thirteen years between 1951 and 1964. The period saw four different prime ministers, Churchill (1951–5), Eden (1955–7), Macmillan (1957–63) and Douglas-Home (1963–4), but there was an essential continuity of policies. During this time the party won three successive general elections (1951, 1955 and 1959), increasing its majority on each occasion, and leading some political commentators to conclude that the Labour Party was in long-term and irreversible decline, with little prospect of again forming a government, as more and more of the population took on the characteristics of the middle class, including a propensity to vote Conservative. Such a pattern might suggest that the electorate, on being offered a clear choice between Conservative and Labour alternatives, decisively endorsed the former and rejected the latter. The reality, however, was somewhat different. Interestingly, before the 1959 campaign took place, a public opinion poll revealed that almost 40 per cent of voters believed that it made no difference which party was in power. The Conservatives were fortunate to hold office at a time of visible affluence. It was a period of conspicuous consumption after the austerity and deprivation of the war years and the immediate post-war era. More and more people were able to afford the trappings of what had previously been thought of as a middle-class lifestyle – home ownership, annual holidays, televisions, washing machines and the like. It was a society well characterized by Macmillan's famous 'never had it so good' remark made at Bedford in 1957 – though Macmillan's words had actually been intended to warn his audience against complacency. Later critics argued that the nation's wealth was misdirected during the 1950s at the expense of the long-term reconstruction and development of British industry. But some sort of material pay-off for the generation which had grown up in the 1930s, fought the war and then lived through the period of post-war austerity was probably a political necessity by this time, whichever party had been in power.

The country was sufficiently contented with its growing prosperity to re-elect the Tories twice. The marginal voter, who determines the outcome of British elections, was happy to see a party which seemed to exude competence carry on. It was precisely because the country seemed, both economically and politically, to be working remarkably well that the population readily accepted the policies of the consensus. 'Change, it was felt, would be wrong, dangerous and unnecessary' (Porter, 1994, p. 294). To the extent that there were underlying problems in the national economy, these were effectively masked as far as most observers were concerned by the upward curve of public expenditure. The apparent success of Keynesian economics, translated into rising living standards, undermined the socialist case for a structural transformation of society just as surely as it ruled out the possibility of a return to the unbridled forces of the free market. Not in fact until the early 1960s did most people feel that all was not well. This is a far more realistic explanation of the electoral history of the 1950s than the idea that the country was emphatically rejecting a markedly different set of options on offer from Labour. There seemed no good reason to change a winning team, particularly when Labour's image was damaged by its own internal disputes and bickering. The decade's cultural landmarks, such as the plays of Wesker and Osborne and films like *Room at the Top*, may give a misleading impression of a society 'caught up in a whirl of popular protest'. A prosperous sense of satisfaction, even complacency, was far more characteristic of the population as a whole (Morgan, 1990, p. 185).

In reality the major improvements in the British economy during this period would probably have occurred irrespective of any policy decisions made by the government. World factors were decisive. The government enjoyed a windfall from two significant changes in the terms of trade. After the end of the Korean War, food and raw material prices fell so dramatically that in 1953 the country could buy 13 per cent more imports than in 1951 for the same amount of exports. A minor world recession in 1957–8 triggered off another, slower slump in commodity prices. Thus the country, along with the industrialized west as a whole, enjoyed a long boom, favourable both to full employment and an expansion of the social services. Perhaps the Conservatives' most significant contribution to the country's economic well-being was to allow the burden of defence spending to fall as a result of increasing reliance on the nuclear deterrent rather than conventional forces. This was the main reason why taxation fell as a proportion of national income for several years running.

Eden's government was overshadowed by questions of foreign policy and especially by the Suez Crisis. So has been, thus far, its examination by historians, but Richard Lamb has suggested that, on the domestic front, Eden was determined to preserve the harmony of the two front benches. Wage-push inflation was showing signs of becoming a serious problem and some economic commentators called for cuts in public spending and a rise in the number out of work. The City felt that a showdown with the trade unions was essential if the wage-price spiral was to be broken, and Lamb concludes that a great opportunity was missed in 1955 for trade union reform, since the moderate union leaders of that time would probably have accepted government measures without too much opposition (Lamb, 1987, pp. 14, 28). This may be an exaggeration. Popular perceptions had not yet placed the problem of inflation sufficiently high on the national agenda to make sweeping legislative changes acceptable. To his credit, however, there is some evidence that Eden was more concerned by inflationary pressures than has usually been appreciated and it is possible that he might have pursued tougher measures to deal with the problem had his premiership not been brought to a premature close by the Suez débâcle (Dutton, 1996, p. 277).

Eden's successor, Macmillan, was even more determined that there should be no return to deflationary policies and pre-Keynesian economics. More perhaps than any post-war prime minister Macmillan epitomized the reality of the consensus. As long ago as 1927 he had co-authored a pamphlet entitled *Industry and the State*, which called for the development of a 'middle way' between unrestrained free enterprise and oppressive socialism. As he wrote in his memoirs, 'encouraged by my old friend, Roy Harrod [biographer of Keynes], I still resisted the idea of deflation as a permanent or even prolonged policy' (Macmillan, 1971, p. 355). But Macmillan's premiership did witness a significant challenge to a central tenet of the post-war consensus, even though it came from within the ranks of his own party rather than the Labour benches opposite. The prime minister's first Chancellor, Peter Thorneycroft, soon became concerned at the ever-rising level of government expenditure and the growing risk of inflation. His warning to the cabinet, delivered as early as January 1957, merits quotation since it is couched in language which did not really enter the mainstream of government thinking for a further twenty years.

> For many years we have had the sorry spectacle of a Government which spends too much, drifts into inflation, then seeks to cure the situation by fiscal and budgetary measures. These attempts in turn lead to flagging production, taxes are reduced, and demand is stimulated; but we shrink from the measures necessary to cut expenditure decisively and inflation starts again. There is only one way out of this unhappy circle, and that is to cut expenditure and not to increase taxation . . . but to reduce it. (quoted in Ramsden, 1996, p. 32)

The Financial Secretary to the Treasury, Enoch Powell, convinced Thorneycroft that inflation could be drastically reduced providing the money supply was brought under control. But such thinking inevitably came up against the orthodoxy of the Keynesian consensus. As Harrod advised the prime minister: 'The idea that you can reduce prices by limiting the quantity of money is pre-Keynesian . . . I do so sincerely hope that no government speaker would use words implying that the Government subscribes to such an antiquated doctrine' (quoted in Lamb, 1995, p. 47). Nevertheless in 1957 Thorneycroft announced his determination to maintain the parity of the pound even if this meant higher unemployment, and before the end of the year he was talking of holding government expenditure at its existing level. The post-war objectives of full employment and economic expansion seemed to be on the brink of being abandoned. Indeed, in September a number of ministers suggested that Thorneycroft's proposals would be interpreted by public opinion as a renunciation of the principles of the 1944 Employment White Paper. But in January 1958, when Macmillan refused to endorse a package of spending cuts, Thorneycroft resigned, taking with him his two junior ministers, Nigel Birch and Enoch Powell. The prime minister dismissed the whole episode as 'a little local difficulty'.

It is now clear that the debate did not end with Thorneycroft's resignation. His two successors, Derick Heathcoat Amory and Selwyn Lloyd, shared his concern over inflation. Amory later recalled a most revealing conversation he had had with the prime minister. ' "What is wrong with inflation, Derry!" I'd reply, "You're thinking of your constituency in the 1930s?" – "Yes, I'm thinking of the under-use of resources – let's over-use them!"' (quoted in Horne, 1989, p. 140). In his 1960 Budget Amory wanted to introduce a mild dose of deflation in order to cool down an overheated economy, but was dissuaded by the prime minister from doing so. In a note written to Macmillan shortly before his retirement from politics in July 1960, Amory insisted that 'price stability' was of paramount importance to the country (Lamb, 1995, p. 68). But despite mounting evidence that inflation was a genuine problem, Macmillan set his face against any suggestion of pro-longed deflation. According to Lloyd, the prime minister's greatest mistake was 'thinking unemployment a worse enemy than uncon-trolled inflation' (quoted in Thorpe, 1989, p. 360). Indeed, Macmillan's underlying idea seems to have been that a limited amount of inflation was tolerable – even desirable – precisely because it provided the necessary excess of cash and credit to fund the growth of the economy. When in 1962 Lloyd, together with a third of the Cabinet, was sacked in Macmillan's famous 'Night of the Long Knives', Nigel Birch wrote cuttingly to *The Times* that 'for the second time the Prime Minister has got rid of a Chancellor of the Exchequer who tried to get expenditure under control. Once is more than enough.' The dispute was basically between those who, like Macmillan, were still haunted by memories of the 1930s, and who firmly held that increased state spending was needed to build a happy and united nation, and those who viewed such a strategy as likely ultimately to lead to economic disaster. In the last resort neither Amory nor Lloyd carried sufficient political weight to win the argument against the prime minister.

Such debates within the Conservative Party caused little more than a ripple on the surface of cross-party consensus. Indeed, the party's manifesto for the 1959 General Election represented the high-water mark of consensual Conservatism. Tory policy was 'to double the standard of living in this generation and to ensure that all sections of society share in the expansion of wealth'. The manifesto's first major legislative commitment was for dealing with high regional unemployment. After the election, the consensus appeared to be moving leftwards again. In the early 1960s the parties competed with one another in their ability to create faster economic growth and then distribute the fruits of that growth. Public spending plans actually grew on the assumption that higher rates of growth could be achieved in the future. Growth became an economic panacea. It would enable the government to spend more on social welfare, while protecting workers' take-home pay. Whereas Conservative rhetoric since 1951 had been permeated with slogans about freedom, Macmillan and Lloyd now seemed ready to achieve growth through planning and controls. 'So far as I am concerned', wrote Macmillan to Lloyd, 'I have no fear of [greater state direction] because these were the policies that I recommended before the war' (quoted in Ramsden, 1996, p. 159). With the setting up of the National Economic Development Council (1961) and the National Incomes Commission (1962), and the introduction of an incomes policy, Conservatism moved nearer to embracing a corporate state and *dirigiste* society than ever before or since. Macmillan saw in a permanent incomes policy the means to maintain his key objectives of full employment, a strong pound and continuous economic growth. Lord Hailsham's appointment in 1963 as minister with special responsibility for the north–east indicated an interventionist policy to deal with regional unemployment. The NEDC ('Neddy') was particularly important in representing an attempt to bring government, unions and management together to plan the future of British industry and promote economic growth for the benefit of all. Whereas such planning had hitherto been associated with Labour, the initiative now came from Macmillan and Lloyd, supported by the Federation of British Industries. After Lloyd's removal in 1962 Macmillan secured in Reginald Maudling a Chancellor more in tune than any of his three predecessors with the prime minister's commitment to growth as the first priority of economic policy.

Notwithstanding these policy initiatives, the Conservative Party rapidly lost its political momentum from 1961 onwards. Above all the government, and particularly the prime minister, lost their reputations for competence which had been so important in winning electoral endorsement during the 1950s. Sustained growth proved unattainable without dangerously overheating the economy. After an expansionist budget in 1961 Lloyd was obliged in July of the same year to bring in a deflationary package including a pay pause, increased taxes and a rise in the Bank Rate. Labour derided the government's economic management as the era of 'stop–go'. A succession of policy reverses – de Gaulle's veto on Britain's application to join the European Economic Community in 1963 was perhaps the most significant – was compounded by a series of spy and sex scandals. In the most notorious, John Profumo, Minister of War, resigned after admitting an affair with a prostitute who had also shared her bed with a Russian diplomat. There was a widespread feeling that the Conservatives had been in power too long. Labour would make great play in the 1964 election with the slogan, 'Thirteen Wasted Years'. Macmillan, whose calm imperturbability and patrician demeanour had once been great assets, now suddenly appeared old and out of touch. In the growing cult of youth, epitomized in the new American president, John F. Kennedy, the prime minister seemed an anachronism. The chaotic circumstances surrounding Macmillan's enforced retirement because of ill-health in October 1963 and the emergence of the Earl of Home as his successor did little for the Conservative Party's public image. Labour was clearly making considerable progress with what might be called the intellectual voter – perhaps for the first time since 1945. The press and the media were becoming vocal critics of the Conservative government. Even the BBC – for long regarded as a friend of the conservative establishment – emerged in a new role, presenting such satirical programmes as *That Was the Week that Was*. The Conservatives' eclipse in the early 1960s was thus as much cultural as political. This situation was skilfully exploited by a revived Labour Party, and particularly its new leader Harold Wilson. Though the Conservatives made a substantial recovery during the year of Alec Douglas-Home's premiership, it was not sufficient to prevent a Labour victory in 1964 by the narrow overall majority of five seats.

In that election voters were apparently offered a clear choice, if only between the former fourteenth earl, transposed reluctantly as Wilson suggested from a Scottish grousemoor, and the Labour leader with his north country accent and exaggeratedly working-class credentials. The down-to-earth modernizing Labour Party seemed to be pitted against the Edwardian langour of the Conservative aristocracy. Yet in policy terms the choice was less clear-cut. In the by-election which brought him back to the House of Commons Sir Alec had emphasized that he had no misgivings about fighting on a policy of higher public expenditure. The *Sunday Telegraph* went so far as to question the wisdom of a Conservative prime minister seeking to 'underplay everything that distinguishes Conservatism from contemporary socialism' (Ramsden, 1996, p. 217). According to David Robertson the election manifestos of the two parties were closer together on the central issue of economic policy than at any time in the previous forty years (Robertson, 1976, p. 98). Labour probably won in 1964 on the successful projection of an image rather than an alternative set of policies. Wilson's basic appeal was that Labour would perform more competently in office than a Conservative Party which had run out of steam after thirteen years in power. It was not dissimilar to the Tories' own case back in 1951. Though Labour's manifesto promised a 'New Britain' there was little sense of an alternative ideology on offer. Wilson's enemy was not so much capitalism as the prevailing amateurism of British society (Searle, 1995, p. 230). It was the machinery for running the country which was to be changed, with emphasis on science and technology to make full use of 'our national wealth in brains, our genius for scientific invention and medical discovery'. Iain Macleod's analysis of the Conservative defeat is instructive: 'For the first time in five elections our grip on the centre has weakened' (Fisher, 1973, p. 259). He himself commented that the welfare proposals in Labour's first Queen's Speech represented 'exactly the policy that one would have liked to see in the Speech if the Tories had won' (Shepherd, 1994, p. 382).

As usually happens when Labour takes office, there were expectations in some quarters that the victory of 1964 would mean a distinct advance towards a socialist society. 'We began to feel that the Left was on its way,' recorded Barbara Castle (Castle, 1984, p. ix). Indeed it was part of Wilson's success as party leader that he was able largely to satisfy his own left wing, some of whom fondly believed that one of their own number now occupied 10 Downing Street. But Wilson was an inherently cautious premier. He proved stronger on rhetoric than genuine ideological conviction. 'Socialism, as I understand it,' he said in 1963, 'means applying a sense of purpose to our national life: economic purpose, social purpose and moral purpose. Purpose means technical skill' (quoted in Kavanagh, 1987, p. 158). If Wilson had ever been truly of the party's left wing, he had moved considerably towards the right since his Bevanite days. His administration proved to be 'a cautious, conservative, tentative Government, deeply suspicious of truly radical departures' (James, 1972, p. 81). With Gaitskell dead and Butler on the brink of political retirement, 'Butskellism' was no longer an appropriate description of the government's economic policy. But, writes Philip Ziegler, 'there were traces of MacWilson to be found in Number 10 in 1964 and 1965' (Ziegler, 1993, p. 198). The new prime minister was not reluctant to make symbolic gestures. Wilson's skill 'was to give the appearance of great changes without in fact making any of substance' (James, 1972, p. 60). Prescription charges were abolished and well-known left wingers, Barbara Castle and Jennie Lee (widow of Aneurin Bevan), were appointed to the new ministries of Overseas Development and the Arts. Neither, of course, was in a position to advance socialism. Even the new Department of Economic Affairs, headed by George

Brown and championing the much heralded National Plan, achieved little and lost much of its authority after 1966. The only measure of nationalization promised in the party's manifesto was the renationalization of steel. 'Of any intention of creating a socialist Britain . . . the 1964 government was entirely innocent' (Campbell, 1987, p. 374). Not surprisingly, there was soon talk of a realignment of Liberal and Labour parties in a non-socialist, moderate, reforming movement of the left.

Inherited financial problems and the narrowness of the government's parliamentary majority gave Wilson good excuses against the charge that he was betraying his socialist mission. Little, however, changed when Labour sought, and received, a clearer electoral mandate in 1966. During that campaign the Liberal Party made effective use of a poster carrying portraits of the Labour and Conservative leaders with the slogan 'Which Twin is the Tory?' Apart from steel renationalization, which had not been achieved in the 1964–6 Parliament because of the fragility of the government's majority, there was little mention of socialism. Despite public apathy on the issue, Wilson knew that the steel pledge would help keep the Left happy. Some reassurance was required that socialism had not been completely discarded.

The rhetoric of inter-party animosity increased during the Wilson years, but this owed much to a personal antipathy between the prime minister and the new Conservative leader, Edward Heath, who succeeded Douglas-Home in 1965. Significantly, Douglas-Home had not been a success as leader of the opposition at least in part because of his unwillingness to attack Labour policies which were not dissimilar from those his own government had pursued in office. As he later confessed, he 'was never very impressed by the Tweedledum and Tweedledee form of politics in the Commons. It didn't make sense . . . to go bashing ahead against a Government's policies, which perhaps had much to commend them, simply to keep backbenchers happy' (Ramsden, 1996, p. 232; Margach, 1978, p. 136). As the 1960s progressed, a growing disdain for Wilson as a political trickster developed on the Conservative benches as a whole. The 1970 Tory manifesto condemned Labour's 'cheap and trivial style of government'. In fact, however, 'Heath and

Wilson shared far more objectives and assumptions than fundamental divides' (Whitehead, 1985, p. 50). Indeed, Heath had been
chosen to replace Douglas-Home as Tory leader at least in part
because he was felt to be a politician in the Wilson mould. By the
time of the General Election of 1970 a *Punch* cartoon showed
Wilson hanging on grimly to the coat-tails of Conservatism as he
moved ever further away from socialism (D. Butler, 1989, p. 26).
Similarly, *The Times* pointed to the difficulty the Conservatives had
in challenging a government which seemed to answer so well the
conservative instincts of the electorate (Ramsden, 1996, p. 308).

In line with the trend of the Conservative government's economic
policy over the previous Parliament, Labour entered office in 1964
convinced that the solution to what was by then seen as a national
economic malaise lay in faster growth and the modernization of
managerial methods. In another of his celebrated phrases, Wilson
spoke of the 'white heat' of technology. Results, however, were
disappointing. For many 'white heat' amounted to little more than
'hot air'. Over the period of Labour government, 1964–70, the
annual average rate of growth was only 2.2 per cent. What was
striking, however, was the way in which the government used
methods and instruments which had their origins in the Macmillan
and Home governments. 'Much of the small print of the 1965
National Plan and Mr. Wilson's own "purposive physical intervention"
had already been enacted before Labour came to power' (Brittan,
1971, p. 290). Brown's advisers at the DEA were Keynesians to a
man. 'The case will no doubt be argued on the basis of Socialist
"planning" versus Tory "freedom"', wrote Iain Macleod of the
National Plan. But 'the argument is sterile and unreal. It was Mr.
Selwyn Lloyd, not Mr. George Brown, who set up the NEDC, and
it is hard to find a single new proposal in the whole 492 pages'
(quoted in Shepherd, 1994, p. 408). The fundamental continuity
was particularly evident after the sterling crisis of 1966. There were
to be no seismic shifts in macro-economic policy.

Wilson's government failed to avoid the basic problem which had
beset the Tories, particularly after the mid–1950s – that attempts
to accelerate growth resulted in higher imports, a balance-of-
payments deficit and a crisis of confidence in sterling, leading to

a period of enforced restraint. In the context of the post-war consensus, Wilson and his Chancellors (James Callaghan 1964–7, and Roy Jenkins, 1967–70) proved to be rigidly orthodox. In the first days of the new administration senior ministers ruled out devaluation as a policy option. During the crisis of 1966 the cabinet, faced with a stark choice between deflation and devaluation, opted for a massive dose of the former. Like its Conservative predecessor, the Labour government placed the defence of sterling and the balance of payments ahead of growth, a strategy which many now believe did lasting damage to the British economy. When devaluation was finally adopted in 1967, it was done as a last resort rather than as a positive policy option. Though Jenkins did much to restore a sound economy, the cost was high in terms of increased taxation and expenditure cuts.

Governmental attitudes towards the trade unions showed an interesting development in the shape of the consensus during the Wilson years. Ever since they had acquired a new legitimacy during the national struggle against Hitler, the unions had been treated with kid gloves and increasingly drawn into a shared responsibility for the management of the economy to defend full employment and promote economic expansion. Governments of both parties had shown a determination to work with rather than against the unions, a process which reached a climax with the creation of the NEDC under Selwyn Lloyd in 1961. 'I for one do not object to the idea of consensus,' declared Lloyd's successor, Reginald Maudling. 'I know of no industrialist who prefers fighting the Trade Unions to working with them where this is possible' (Maudling, 1978, p. 141). From the late 1950s, however, the unions began to suffer a decline in popular esteem. They were thought to be too powerful and yet not able to control the actions of their own members, with the unofficial wildcat strike led by unrepresentative, militant, left-wing shop stewards becoming a particular bogy in the public mind. At all events, the unions' capacity for damage was thought to be excessive. Such feelings were encouraged by the succession of a new generation of union leaders such as Frank Cousins, Hugh Scanlon and Jack Jones, whose political views were decidedly to the left of those of their predecessors.

During the Wilson years the problem became acute. In the two years 1963–4 about four million working days were lost through strikes. In the two years 1968–9 the total had increased to about 11.5 million. The Labour government itself believed that the damaging dock strike of 1967, which Wilson condemned as being politically inspired, was a major factor in making devaluation unavoidable. Opinion polls showed that there was considerable popular support for a policy of placing legal curbs on the unions and the government's failure to act so far was seen as the most important single factor in explaining the collapse of Wilson's personal 'satisfaction' rating from 69 per cent in 1966 to 33 per cent in January 1969 (Ziegler, 1993, p. 299). The government's opportunity came with the publication of the report of a Royal Commission under Lord Donovan in June 1968. Its conclusions were less than radical but offered the prime minister the chance to seize the initiative in the hope of regaining credibility with the electorate (Pimlott, 1992, p. 528). With the thinking of the Conservative Party moving in the same direction, it was in many ways a high point of the post-war consensus that it should have been a Labour government, and more particularly the one-time Bevanite, Harold Wilson, and his new Employment Secretary, the left-winger, Barbara Castle, who determined in 1969 to introduce a legal framework into industrial relations. This was despite the fact that the majority on the Donovan Commission had decisively rejected any form of legal sanctions to enforce industrial discipline. The government's proposals, embodied in the White Paper *In Place of Strife*, were not a carbon copy of the Conservative document, *Fair Deal at Work*, but there were some striking similarities. The Tories had proposed a sixty-day cooling-off period for certain strikes, the registration of unions and a clearer definition of what constituted a trade dispute. Labour's was a balanced package which would have given the trade unions considerable advantages including, for the first time, the statutory right to belong to a trade union, in return for accepting certain binding obligations. Mrs Castle has always maintained that her proposals were designed to *strengthen* the trade unions and the *quid pro quo* which she demanded in return – that 'the unions should co-operate in avoiding unnecessary strikes' – was a modest one (Castle, 1993, p. 417). But the unions themselves were outraged by the proposal which would have enabled the Secretary of State to require those involved in a dispute to desist from strike action for up to twenty-eight days. Vic Feather, General Secretary of the TUC, claimed that the suggested legislation would have introduced 'the taint of criminality' into industrial relations.

Opposition was not confined to the trade unions themselves. Inside the Parliamentary Labour Party and within the cabinet itself (with James Callaghan leading the rebels), objections mounted. Tony Benn, who had begun by supporting the proposals, recorded the change of mood: 'There is growing anxiety in the Cabinet, and I am now joining the anxious group, fearing that an Industrial Relations Bill just can't work' (Benn, 1988, p. 186). The prime minister declared that the proposed legislation was 'an essential component of ensuring the economic success of the Government'. Its passage was vital to its continuance in office – 'there can be no going back on that'. In the end, however, Wilson was virtually isolated inside his own cabinet. He could not even look to the Tories for help. The latter offered no lifeline because they sensed that the hated Wilson was now on the run – an interesting example of the way in which a consensus on policy is often obscured in the British system by the necessities of the political game and sheer personal animosity. Eventually Wilson and Castle had to give way, and on 18 June 1969 they accepted a face-saving formula in which the TUC General Council issued a 'solemn and binding undertaking' that its member unions would observe the TUC's own guidelines on unofficial strikes. One cabinet minister joked about 'Mr Soloman Binding' and the tag inevitably stuck. But this could not disguise the general interpretation of what had happened which was that Wilson had capitulated totally to the overweening power of the trade union movement. As will be seen, this was an important date in the ultimate demise of the post-war consensus. Wilson had let go a unique opportunity to tip the balance of industrial relations marginally in favour of management in a way that could have had 'untold consequences for the future cost of labour and, through that, for all-round economic health' (Hennessy and Seldon, 1987, p. 199).

Not surprisingly, there was little open conflict between the major parties on foreign and defence policies between 1964 and 1970. Division was far more apparent within Labour's own ranks. Labour's course proved to be strikingly similar to that which would have been charted by a Conservative government, though the essential continuity was sometimes disguised by Wilson's propensity for newsworthy initiatives. Wilson's three appointees as Foreign Secretary – Patrick Gordon-Walker, Michael Stewart and George Brown – were all drawn from the right of the party. The prime minister's official biographer notes that he trusted Stewart because he always knew where he would stand, 'which was usually somewhere to the right of any but the most immoderate Tory' (Ziegler, 1993, p. 173). Labour's 1964 manifesto declared of the country's nuclear deterrent, whose retention had been a cardinal feature in the Conservative programme: 'It will not be independent and it will not be British and it will not deter.' Yet in office both the deterrent and loyalty to the United States remained cornerstones of Labour's foreign policy. Wilson even failed to distance himself significantly from America's growing involvement in the Vietnam War, much to the outrage of his own left wing. The left was also shocked by the cabinet's decision in November 1964 to meet existing arms orders for the apartheid regime in South Africa, by Britain's support for the federal government in the Nigerian Civil War and by the physical removal of the inhabitants of the tiny island of Diego Garcia in the Indian Ocean to make way for an American military base. Research has shown that Wilson's subservience to the United States was in part due to a bargain struck with President Johnson whereby America agreed to prop up the value of the pound sterling (Ponting, 1989, pp. 48–9).

There were some minor reductions in British commitments. Some defence projects, such as the TSR 2 aircraft and a fifth Polaris submarine, were dropped, but overall little changed, with Britain maintaining a significant defence presence east of Suez. This was scarcely surprising for anyone who took note of Wilson's Mansion House speech in November 1964, in which the prime minister declared, 'We are a world power and a world influence or we are nothing.' This, commented the American correspondent Drew

Middleton, 'sounds like any Tory statement' (quoted in Childs, 1986, p. 170). Two years later Wilson could still maintain that Britain's frontier was on the Himalayas. Only in 1968, and under the impact of compelling financial expediency rather than any socialist beliefs, did the government embark on a serious and wide-ranging reappraisal of the country's grossly over-extended defence liabilities, a process which led to the effective abandonment of any military role east of Suez. Even then, military expenditure remained at a very high level and continued to include the so-called independent nuclear deterrent (Morgan, 1990, p. 283).

The increasing hollowness of Britain's supposed status as a world power was one of the factors which persuaded Wilson to change course on the issue of Europe. At the time of Macmillan's abortive application for membership of the EEC, the Labour Party under Gaitskell had been divided but on balance hostile. Membership, suggested Gaitskell, would mean 'the end of Britain as an independent nation state . . . the end of a thousand years of history' (Williams, 1979, p. 407). Wilson, however, encouraged by such pro-Europeans in his cabinet as George Brown and Roy Jenkins, came to the conclusion that in a rapidly changing world Britain's future lay in Europe. The multi-racial Commonwealth had long been a Labour ideal, and a possible alternative to closer integration with Europe. But the 1960s were a time of mounting disillusion-ment with the legacy of Britain's imperial past. As the newly independent members of the Commonwealth increasingly aban-doned British ways and ideals, a rapid reappraisal took place in Labour's ranks. *Faute de mieux* a European future seemed the only option. Wilson's application in 1967 proved as futile as Macmillan's had been in the face of de Gaulle's steadfast and highly individu-alistic opposition to British membership. But its importance in the present context is that the consensus had been maintained, albeit somewhat precariously in view of the deep-seated misgivings on the Labour benches, and in very different terms from that which had existed on the European issue in the period 1945–57.

On the question of education the post-war consensus seemed likely to break down on the issue of selection for secondary schools. After 1966 the government went ahead with plans to implement a comprehensive scheme. The majority of Conservative MPs wanted a clear opposition to this policy and defence of the grammar schools, but it is noticeable that the Tory spokesman, Sir Edward Boyle, with Heath's support, was more guarded in his reaction. Though opposing compulsion, Boyle favoured the comprehensive principle and the ending of selection at the age of eleven. When the Conservatives returned to power, it was their Secretary of State for Education, Margaret Thatcher, who ensured that the drive towards comprehensivization continued. She approved more schemes for comprehensives and the abolition of more grammar schools than any other holder of her office.

A considerable amount of progressive, some would say permissive, social legislation on issues such as capital punishment, abortion and homosexuality reached the statute book during the lifetime of Wilson's government. It was legislation which might well not have succeeded under a Conservative administration. But most of it derived from back-bench initiatives rather than government proposals. On occasions the government behaved in a far less liberal fashion, as when, in 1968, it hurriedly passed restrictive immigration legislation when confronted with the prospect of a wave of East African Asians entering the country. The first controls over Commonwealth immigration had been introduced by the Conservatives in 1962. Labour had been pledged to repeal this measure, but in practice tightened existing restrictions.

Not surprisingly, by the time Wilson's government came to an end in 1970, the Labour left felt profoundly disillusioned. It was not only that the cause of socialism had not been advanced. With the management of the economy becoming ever more difficult, Labour had had to reintroduce prescription charges, postpone plans to raise the school-leaving age and increase charges for school meals. The building of new homes had declined, while the numbers out of work increased. The 'pragmatism' upon which Wilson had once placed great virtue seemed to have degenerated into a series of crisis expedients, devoid of any real strategy to cope with the growing problems of the national economy. On top of this were such 'Tory' measures as wage restraint, proposed curbs on trade unions, immigration controls and support for American 'imperialism' in Vietnam. Tony Benn recorded that it was during this period that 'my own radicalisation took shape, and I began . . . to formulate policies which were more explicitly democratic and socialist' (Benn, 1988, p. xii). On the other hand, if Labour activists felt depressed, Conservatives could not even claim that Wilson had made a success of consensus politics. The great strength of the post-war consensus had been its apparent capacity to deliver continuing material prosperity. Now even that seemed to be in doubt. It was in these circumstances that Edward Heath entered Downing Street, pledged 'to change the course of history of this nation, nothing less'. After a quarter of a century it seemed that the consensus might be about to collapse.

4

The Consensus Challenged, 1970–9

The 1960s proved a disappointing decade as far as the performance of the British economy was concerned. It is scarcely surprising, therefore, that it was in this area that the post-war consensus first began to break down. In a revealing comment, Keith Joseph once remarked that 'the seeds of break in the consensus were being continuously implanted by disappointed expectations' (Joseph, 1987, p. 28). As has been seen, governments of both political parties had, since about 1947, pursued broadly Keynesian policies. The apparent problem by the 1960s was the inability of a Keynesian approach to produce growth, full employment *and* a stable level of prices (Marquand, 1988, ch 2). In retrospect it is not certain that all policies pursued since the establishment of the consensus had been truly Keynesian. After all, Keynes himself had died in 1946. Prophetically, he himself had once remarked that 'all politicians are the slaves of some defunct economist'. His writings had prescribed remedies for the economic conditions of the 1930s and 1940s and it is by no means clear that he would have agreed with subsequent interpretations of his ideas applied to the 1950s and 1960s. Almost certainly Keynes would have taken a more concerned view of the problem of inflation than did some of his later disciples. Whether he would have had an answer to that problem is another matter. In June 1945 he confessed, 'One is also, simply because one knows no solution, inclined to turn a blind eye to the wages problem in a full employment economy' (quoted in Cairncross, 1985, p. 16).

Typically, economists who professed to be Keynesians were willing to risk price rises of around 2 or 3 per cent per annum in order to remove the danger of a deficiency of demand and therefore unemployment. Unfortunately, policies of economic expansion regularly resulted in a balance-of-payments deficit as imports were sucked into the country. This led in turn to pressure on the country's foreign currency reserves and on the exchange rate. Because politicians of both parties continually argued that 'sterling must have first priority', the response was then temporarily to deflate the economy in order to demonstrate prudent financial management to the international money markets. During Selwyn Lloyd's time as Chancellor this strategy achieved notoriety as the tactics of 'stop–go'. But previous chancellors had experienced similar difficulties. Thorneycroft's resignation in 1958 has already been noted. Even earlier, Butler's 1955 budget had been an overtly electioneering measure. It had allowed the economy to get overheated, with the result that corrective measures were necessary once the election was out of the way. Many would now look to this time, reinforced by Monckton's concessions to the unions, as the moment when the inflationary wage spiral first began to get hold of the post-war economy (Horne, 1988, p. 378).

Contemporaries, however, took comfort in the belief that, with only a little pain, they could always bring the situation back under control. According to the so-called Phillips Curve, the government could trade off price stability against a slowdown in economic expansion. Minor adjustments in demand management would reduce inflation at the cost of a small rise in unemployment. Thus it was thought possible to manage the economy by choosing between different amounts of inflation and unemployment, depending on the situation at the time. But by the end of the Wilson government it was clear that the British economy could experience rising inflation *and* rising unemployment at the same time. The complacency of the 1950s was replaced by a discernible feeling that things were 'not quite right' in the Britain of the 1960s (Dorey, 1995, p. 67). The term stagflation was coined to describe a combination of low growth, rising unemployment and inflation. Pulling the levers according to instruction no longer produced the desired result. Inflation averaged only 3.5 per cent during the first half of the 1960s. Between 1968 and 1970, however, retail prices rose by an average of 5.9 per cent per year, partly as a consequence of the inflationary effects of the Vietnam War. Between 1970 and 1973 the average annual increase was running at 8.6 per cent. During the same period there was a worrying increase in the numbers out of work. During the Wilson government of 1964–70 unemployment increased from 376,000 to 555,000. In 1972 it touched the psychologically important one million mark: 'Keynesian economics faced something of an intellectual crisis' (Kavanagh, 1987, p. 125).

The *relative* strength of the British economy was also giving cause for concern. The slow rate of British growth compared most unfavourably with that of some of the founder members of the EEC, particularly West Germany and France, though in reality this was part of a much longer-term problem going back to the last century (Marquand, 1988). Britain's annual rate of growth between 1955 and 1964 averaged just 2.8 per cent. In the same period the corresponding figures for Italy, France, Germany and Japan were 5.4 per cent, 5.4 per cent, 5.7 per cent and 13.6 per cent respectively. The British share of the world trade in manufactured goods fell from 19.8 per cent to 13.9 per cent in the same period and in so-called 'invisibles' from 24.9 per cent to 17.9 per cent (Porter, 1994, p. 304). As the *Lloyds Bank Review* put it in July 1961, 'anyone who can rest content with Britain's economic performance in the 1950s compared with those of other leading industrial nations must have set his sights desperately low in the late 1940s' (quoted in Coopey, Fielding and Tiratsoo, 1993, p. 19). In the early 1960s, while the British economy was beset by a series of balance of payments crises, those of competitor countries were surging ahead. The balance of payments was in the red for three years out of five up to 1964. Between 1952 and 1959 it had been in constant surplus. By the early 1960s many were coming to realize that the notion of Britain as the world's third great power no longer had much meaning. Indeed, most converts to the idea of British membership of the European Community, on which issue a new consensus had been established by 1967, were moved by the straightforward desire to see Britain emulate her continental rivals, rather than by any deep-seated Europeanism.

It was the Conservative Party which made the first significant attacks on the post-war consensus. Of the Treasury ministers who resigned in 1958 it was Enoch Powell who emerged as the most articulate exponent of that libertarian, free-market Conservatism which had been largely submerged since the late 1940s. Powell contested the party leadership in 1965 on a right-wing platform when the two front runners, Edward Heath and Reginald Maudling, were firmly identified with those left-of-centre policies which had dominated Conservative thinking for the previous two decades. His tally of just fifteen votes was a fair indication of the balance of forces within the party at that time, but it was worthy of note that his supporters included two MPs – John Biffen and Nicholas Ridley – who were to figure prominently in Mrs Thatcher's cabinets in the 1980s. Particularly after his refusal to serve under Home in 1963 and again after his dismissal from Heath's shadow cabinet in 1968, Powell used his back-bench freedom to attack state management of the economy and to argue that government was the sole originator of inflation through its excessive spending. Powell rejected state intervention in the economy as being without benefit and argued that the post-war consensus had forced 'even a Tory Government to operate within the framework of an explicitly Socialist public opinion' (Ramsden, 1996, p. 277). 'Upon the sound working of the money system', he wrote in 1969, 'and above all upon the stability and honesty of the currency, depend not only the operation of industry and commerce but . . . the structure of society itself' (quoted in H. Young, 1989, p. 61). To begin with, Powell's free-market, monetary policies were usually dismissed as an unrealistic throwback to the *laissez-faire* philosophy of the nineteenth century.

Another sign that the consensus was not universally endorsed was the foundation of the right-wing Monday Club in 1961. Its members were dismayed by Macmillan's famous 'Wind of Change' speech of February 1960, in which the prime minister had drawn attention to the imminent demise of European colonialism.

Opposed to the liberal consensus on coloured immigration, they believed that under the influence of men such as Butler and Macmillan Conservatism had moved so far to the left that there was little to choose between the two major parties. Apart from attacking Labour's competence to govern, there seemed no scope for genuine party differentiation. Though they never fully coalesced, influences such as Powell and the Monday Club helped to move the party's position to the right after the election defeat of 1964. To continue with policies virtually indistinguishable from Labour's only made sense if the electorate continued to vote for the Conservative version of the consensus. Once in opposition the Conservatives had little room for manoeuvre except by moving to the right, if the electorate was ever going to be offered a real choice again. The grass roots seemed ready to change direction. In 1965 the party's London Area demanded 'an assurance that the next Conservative government will govern by true Conservative principles, not seeking electoral popularity by the adoption of quasi-Socialist measures' (Ramsden, 1996, p. 219). The following year North Cornwall Tories declared that there was 'little to choose between Socialist and present Conservative policies' and urged a return to 'real Conservative principles with a far greater emphasis on individual freedom' (Ramsden, 1996, p. 255). The change was apparent in the policy document *Putting Britain Right Ahead*, published in October 1965. With little mention of NEDC or incomes policies, it stressed ideas of competition and incentives, a shift from direct to indirect taxation and greater selectivity in the provision of social services, all of which seemed to mark a conscious break with the past.

Much of this new thinking was embraced in the Conservative manifesto for the 1966 General Election, *Action not Words*. There were proposals to reduce income tax, offer greater incentives to managers, break up monopolies, increase competition, join the EEC and move towards a more selective provision of welfare benefits. Much of this foreshadowed the Conservatism of Keith Joseph and Margaret Thatcher. But there was an important difference. Though the party had moved distinctly to the right, and while many now thought Butskellism was dead as far as the Conservative Party was concerned, the motive force was practical rather than ideological. Heath, who had taken a large personal part in the policy rethink, was himself firmly in the 'One Nation' tradition of post-war Conservatism. 'I never have been a laissez-faire Tory at any time in my life', he insisted in 1973. According to Keith Joseph, Heath's government of 1970 still adopted 'a statist approach, though with a huge emphasis on releasing entrepreneurship, on reforming trade unions and on sharpening competition' (Joseph, 1987, p. 28). James Prior, who also served in the Heath cabinet, confirmed that the government remained 'strongly committed to the post-war economic and social consensus in which the basic goal of economic policy was full employment' (Prior, 1986, p. 71). The new policies reflected Heath's belief that Britain was sliding remorselessly downhill and that drastic action was necessary to reverse the trend. 'It was the product not of right-wing ideology, but of an efficiency expert' (Lindsay and Harrington, 1979, p. 244). Indeed, Heath was the very reverse of an ideologue. His philosophy was that of a manager. According to Douglas Hurd, who worked closely with him at this time, Heath and his close colleagues spent little time justifying their actions in terms of ideas (Hurd, 1979, p. 91). Enoch Powell confirmed that Heath was reluctant to debate concepts rather than policies (Ramsden, 1996, p. 254). With the single exception of the need for British membership of the European Economic Community – a consistent theme throughout his long career – Heath was not motivated by burning convictions about specific policies. 'Are you moving at all to the right?' a friend is said to have asked Heath in 1970. 'Just a bit,' he replied, 'but we have to stay in the centre' (quoted in Whitehead, 1985, p. 40). Significantly, it was crucial to Heath's plans that government ministries, local government and the NHS should all be restructured in the interests of efficiency.

Seldom, if ever, in the twentieth century has a prospective government prepared its policies so thoroughly as Heath's Conservative Party did before the 1970 General Election. After the 1966 election there was considerable debate within the party on the question of an incomes policy, with the majority now siding with Enoch Powell in the belief that this was not a proper function of government. But a minority around Reginald Maudling clung to the view that an incomes policy would remain an important weapon for a future Tory government in the fight against inflation. The failure of Labour's *In Place of Strife* in 1969 opened up a significant rift between the parties on how to deal with the power of the trade unions. It became for a time the deepest point of conflict between Labour and the Conservatives, with the latter determined to press on where Labour had drawn back and introduce a legal framework into industrial relations. Such a policy attracted even many on the left of the Tory Party since, deprived of incomes policies, they saw curbing the unions as one of the few options available to keep wage inflation under control. With a growing sense of personal antipathy, particularly between their leaders, the two parties seemed to be moving away from their commitments to consensus.

The retirement of Edward Boyle from front-bench politics in 1969 was symbolic of the Conservatives' move to the right. Boyle was the epitome of the sort of left-of-centre Toryism which had dominated the party's inner councils for at least two decades. He seemed to espouse all the progressive causes which the Conservative right most disliked. It was equally symbolic – though more in hindsight than at the time – that his replacement as Shadow Education Secretary should have been Mrs Margaret Thatcher (Ramsden, 1996, p. 299). Even so, the gap between Conservatives and Labour was still not as wide as party rhetoric suggested. A shadow cabinet in which Iain Macleod, Reginald Maudling and Quintin Hogg were Heath's three main spokesmen on domestic issues still seemed, in many ways, rooted to the centre ground. In a 1967 report the Director of the Conservative Research Department pointed to the dangers ahead. 'If the Labour Government now moves to the left,' he asserted, 'our task of winning the next election should not be too difficult.' On the other hand, problems would arise if Labour 'attempt to continue in control of the centre'. Much of the present boredom with politics, he warned, 'comes because people cannot distinguish any question of principle between the two main parties' (Coopey, Fielding and Tiratsoo, 1993, p. 192). Yet Labour resolutely refused to abandon the centre ground. Shortly before the General Election of 1970 the *Sunday Times* concluded that Wilson was a pragmatist whose aim was 'to turn

Labour from being a party of protest into a party of power' by offering the electorate 'a distinctly non-doctrinaire style of government' (quoted in Pimlott, 1992, p. 557).

Members of Heath's shadow cabinet met to put the finishing touches to their policies amid a glare of publicity at Selsdon Park in January 1970. Little emerged that had not been said before, apart perhaps from a renewed emphasis on tougher law and order measures. Yet it was surely significant that, when Iain Macleod, as Shadow Chancellor, proposed dismantling the structure of state economic influence such as pay boards, built up by Conservative and Labour governments alike, only three members of the shadow cabinet voiced their dissent (Walker, 1977, pp. 54–5). Wilson, seeing electoral advantage in emphasizing the extent of political polarization, was able to make great play with the idea of 'Selsdon Man' – the hard-hearted face of the new Conservatism, a reactionary opponent of social welfare and the planned economy. In February 1970 the prime minister declared, 'It is not just a lurch to the Right, it is an atavistic desire to reverse the course of 25 years of social revolution. What they are planning is a wanton, calculated and deliberate return to greater inequality. The new Conservative slogan is: Back to the free for all' (James, 1972, p. 214).

It is, then, not surprising that some controversy has developed about the extent to which Heath's Conservative Party set out consciously to break away from the post-war consensus, a controversy that has been heightened by Heath's apparent abandonment of many of the policies upon which he had campaigned half-way through his administration and by an on-going and sometimes bitter debate among Conservatives about the relationship between the Heath and Thatcher governments. According to his biographer, Heath remained more faithful to the One-Nation Tory principles which he had espoused in his first years in Parliament than has always been recognized, while his government pursued a more consistent underlying course than is immediately apparent. John Campbell argues that it was for tactical reasons that Heath's speeches became 'harsher, more overtly capitalistic, less socially conciliatory'. The change remained, however, 'largely window dressing' (Campbell, 1993, p. 246). By the time of the meeting at

Selsdon Park Heath had thus 'allowed himself to be identified with ideas and attitudes which were not really his own' (Campbell, 1993, p. 266). He was 'going along with an aggressively free-market rhetoric which he did not in his heart accept. His purpose . . . was not fundamentally to change the Government's role in relation to the economy' (Campbell, 1993, p. 267). In his later years, motivated above all by his detestation of his successor as Conservative leader, Heath has missed no opportunity to stress that his own credentials as a Tory belong with the traditions of Butler and Macmillan and not with those of Mrs Thatcher.

Certainly, the party's 1970 manifesto contained small print and reservations which, carefully studied, might have modified the ardour and expectations of the free-marketeers. But if Heath's move to the right really was entirely of rhetoric and not substance, his tactics were probably too successful for his own good. It is clear that the party's right-wing was enthused by what was going on. 'When [Heath] took his Shadow Cabinet to the Selsdon Park Hotel . . . and produced the new policies on which he would fight the election', recalled Nicholas Ridley, 'I became enthusiastic' (Ridley, 1991, p. 3). Norman Tebbit, elected to parliament for the first time in 1970, was of the same mind. 'No one should doubt that at the time of the election in 1970 Ted Heath was committed to the end of that corporate consensus and to the new liberal economics' (Tebbit, 1988, p. 94). When the Heath government did change course, with for example the introduction in 1972 of a statutory incomes policy, even those at the heart of the government conceded that this was 'a complete reversal of the declared policies of the 1970 manifesto' (Whitelaw, 1989, p. 125). If, then, Heath had not actually determined by 1970, as an act of policy, to break the post-war consensus, it seems hard to deny that this was the thrust of the programme which he now placed before the electorate.

Against the predictions of most opinion polls, Heath became prime minister in June 1970 with a comfortable overall majority of thirty seats. The new government seemed determined to give the country policies that were fundamentally different from any seen since 1945. The new Conservatism was intended to be bracing and stimulating. For the individual there would be more take-home pay, but he would also have to do more for himself. Only those who could not would be protected by a safety net of selective benefits. Such corporate agencies as the Industrial Reorganization Corporation and the Prices and Incomes Board were quickly dismantled. Whatever Heath's true intentions, the government seemed to be more right-wing than any since before the war, particularly after the sudden death of Iain Macleod, the Chancellor of the Exchequer, only a month after the General Election. The feeling that the government was determined to set the country on a very different path was confirmed by Heath's speech to the party conference a few months after his election triumph. 'If we are to achieve this task', he argued, 'we shall have to bring about a change so radical, a revolution so quiet, and yet so total, that it will go far beyond the programme for a Parliament to which we are committed and on which we have already embarked. We are laying the foundations but they are the foundations for a generation.' It was in economic and industrial policy that the change was most marked. The new government hoped to reduce public expenditure and opposed wage and price regulation, together with excessive state intervention in industry. The tone was set in a speech at the party conference in November 1970 by John Davies, catapulted as a consequence of Macleod's death to the new super-ministry of Trade and Industry. Davies clearly believed he was embarking on an industrial policy to break the post-war consensus of planning and intervention: 'I will not bolster up or bail out companies where I can see no end to the process of propping them up.' Government would no longer rush to the rescue of industrial lame ducks. Anthony Barber's first budget in October 1970 combined substantial cuts in personal and company taxation with reductions in government expenditure on the social services and industry.

Reform of the trade unions was crucial to Heath's plans in order to sweep away ancient restrictive practices which were impeding the performance of British industry. But it was never part of Heath's plan to destroy the unions as a power within the land as, arguably, Mrs Thatcher sought to do after 1979. Heath wanted to place the unions within a legal framework, but was then willing to recognize their importance in the proper functioning of a modern industrial state. Although the Industrial Relations Bill of 1971 was similar in many ways to that envisaged by Wilson and Castle in 1969, the Labour Party opposed it vehemently. Introduced by Robert Carr, it proposed the setting up of a National Industrial Relations Court which would have the power to order pre-strike ballots and to enforce a compulsory cooling-off period of up to sixty days in instances where industrial action would cause critical damage to the economy or the community. The bill took up 450 hours of parliamentary time. In practice, however, the new act proved unworkable. It had been poorly drafted and had little hope of acceptance in the atmosphere of the early 1970s. The trade unions were largely able to ignore its provisions simply by refusing to register under the act, a development which the government seems not to have foreseen.

Despite the careful preparation of the years in opposition, most of Heath's policies went badly wrong. Membership of the EEC was secured – at a heavy price – in 1973, but as far as the economy was concerned all the vital indicators continued to move in the wrong direction. Industrial relations had never been worse in the whole post-war era and the government was humiliated by the miners' strike of 1972. Heath was particularly shaken when unemployment reached one million early in 1972. In general Heath's experience showed the extent to which the effective management of the national economy in the modern era lies outside the control of any government and at the mercy of international forces.

As early as 1971 a massive U-turn was under way. A mini-budget in July marked a turning point in the sense that the reduction of unemployment had once more replaced the curbing of inflation as the primary goal of the government's economic policy. Rolls Royce, in difficulties over supplying engines for the Lockheed RB 211 aircraft, was nationalized. Early in 1972 the same remedy was applied to the ailing Upper Clyde Shipbuilders, after the government was warned that failure to do so could lead to public disorder. Trade union leaders were now urged to behave like partners of the prime minister, in a manner not dissimilar to that which the Opposition was currently proposing for a future Labour government. The budget of 1972 cut taxation and allowed public expenditure and government borrowing to rise. The Chancellor, Anthony Barber, announced the setting up of an Industrial Development Executive with powers to inject money into industrial investment. Changes at the Department of Trade and Industry in a ministerial reshuffle in April seemed to symbolize Heath's change of course. The two junior ministers who had been most closely identified with a market-orientated approach were both removed – Sir John Eden to the less politically sensitive Ministry of Posts and Telecommunications, Nicholas Ridley to the backbenches. By August a powerfully interventionist Industry Bill was on the statute book, a complete reversal of the policy upon which the government had been elected. When John Davies introduced the new bill he was greeted with applause from the Labour opposition and an embarrassed silence on the government benches. The new act allowed the minister four times as much discretionary spending power as the Labour provisions which had been abolished in 1970. As Tony Benn put it, here was the 'spadework for socialism' (Ramsden, 1996, p. 352). By the end of the year a formal incomes policy was in operation. In horror at what he regarded as a betrayal of the manifesto upon which the Conservatives had been elected, Enoch Powell brutally demanded to know whether, 'in introducing a compulsory control on wages and prices in contravention of the deepest commitments of this Party, [Heath had] taken leave of his senses?' (quoted in Cosgrave, 1989, p. 297). It was as if a government, which had had the temerity to deviate from the centre ground, was now rushing back to the consensus politics of the early 1960s as fast as it could travel. Public expenditure now reached new heights. In education and the health service, both traditionally regarded as Labour priorities, spending exceeded that of the previous Labour government. In May 1973 an editorial in the Conservative journal *Crossbow* noted that nothing now remained of Selsdon Man. The 1972 budget tax cuts were designed to achieve an annual growth rate of 5 per cent, way in excess of anything achieved since the war. Barber's dash for growth resembled the policy of the last Conservative government, though its consequences proved even more inflationary. By the autumn of 1973 the money supply was increasing at a rate of 27 per cent per annum. It was, argues Kenneth Morgan, a 'kind of Keynesian pump-priming gone mad' (Morgan, 1990, p. 352).

Despite its change of course, success still eluded Heath's government. In a further change of policy in November and December 1973 interest rates were raised to record levels, public expenditure cuts announced and the so-called 'corset' controls on bank lending introduced. Buffeted by the Arab-Israeli war that October and the subsequent quadrupling of the price of oil, the government finally collapsed amidst the ignominy of the three-day week and another defeat at the hands of the miners. But the circumstances of Heath's fall would be of long-term importance for the consensus.

The years after 1970 also saw important developments inside the Labour Party. Not for the first time in its history the party moved distinctly to the left during its period of opposition, abandoning many of the policies pursued by the last Wilson government. The trend was particularly marked in the party outside Parliament, which seemed to be gaining greater influence in the party's decision-making processes. The left-wing Campaign for Labour Party Democracy held its first meeting at the 1973 party conference. Also important was the gradual emergence over a considerable period of time of a new generation of more independent-minded, left-wing trade union leaders, reflecting the views of increasingly militant shop stewards and very unlike the cautious right-wingers who had given their backing to the Attlee government immediately after the war. Tony Benn's chairmanship of the party in 1971–2 was the decisive period. Hitherto regarded as a Gaitskellite centrist, Benn now emerged as a populist champion of the Left, speaking out for more public ownership, greater worker participation in industry and unilateral nuclear disarmament. The Left was able to argue that if Wilson's government had tried to practise the revisionist socialism of Anthony Crosland, it could scarcely claim to have done so successfully. Thus both Labour's failures in government in the 1960s and the Tories' perceived movement to the right offered the Labour Party the opportunity to adopt a more explicitly socialist stance. By 1975 Stuart Holland's *The Challenge of Socialism* had produced a left-wing critique of Crosland's analysis. The Left seemed to be gaining the intellectual ascendancy to a greater degree than at any time since the early 1930s (Seyd, 1987, pp. 24–5).

Within a year of electoral defeat in 1970 the Labour Party as a whole had moved strongly against the EEC, although the leadership continued to stress that the terms of membership negotiated would be the critical factor. The Left was able to argue that there would be little scope for British socialism inside what was seen as a European capitalist club. Wilson seized upon Benn's idea of a future referendum on British membership – an idea which he had previously rejected – as a device to maintain party unity. It was only partially successful, leading to the resignation of Roy Jenkins from the deputy leadership in April 1972. Fellow right-wingers, George Thomson, Harold Lever, David Owen and Dick Taverne, also gave up their front-bench portfolios. This represented a considerable reverse for the long-term ascendancy of social democracy within Labour's ranks, and seems in retrospect something of a dress-rehearsal for the defection of the SDP a decade later. With the Right in some disarray, the Labour Left could make the running in a way that had not been possible in earlier years.

In reaction to the Heath government's Industrial Relations Act, a liaison committee was set up in 1972 between the unions, the party's National Executive Committee and the parliamentary party. This produced the so-called Social Contract by which the unions promised to co-operate in controlling wages in return for government action on prices and a 'social wage' in terms of increased welfare benefits and other reforms. An enthusiast noted: 'The only way was to turn [trade union bargaining] power into something more positive by involving unions in the responsibilities of economic management' (Castle, 1980, p. 9). It was a bargain struck very much on the unions' terms and reflected the advance which the Left had made. 'Labour's Programme for Britain', published in 1972, and 'Labour's Programme 1973' set forth the party's most radical agenda since the war, centred on a National Enterprise Board and a system of compulsory planning agreements with private industry. After a meeting of the NEC in May 1973 Benn recorded his sense of satisfaction. 'The party is now firmly launched on a left-wing policy.' It was, he said, 'a remarkable development of views that we have achieved in three years of hard work' (Benn, 1989, pp. 42–3). Under the next Labour government the frontiers of state ownership would make their first substantial advance since the late 1940s. Though Wilson narrowly avoided a commitment to take over twenty-five leading companies, Labour now promised a fundamental and irreversible shift in the distribution of wealth to working people and their families. By the time of the February 1974 General Election the party was committed not only to a major extension of public ownership, but also to a new Wealth Tax and massive increases in the welfare services.

Not surprisingly, the movement away from the centre ground in first the Conservative Party (1965–72) and then Labour (1970–4) resulted in a marked period of adversarial politics. Opposition for opposition's sake seemed to be the order of the day and there was a bitterness in political debate which made it difficult to imagine that the consensus was still in being. Even in areas traditionally regarded as beyond the scope of party political divisions the consensus seemed to be breaking down. The Northern Ireland problem, where the two front benches had hitherto been scrupulous in maintaining a bipartisan approach, was a case in point. In November 1971, Wilson put forward a controversial plan for a 'fifteen year period of transition' to a united Ireland. Another inevitable consequence was a revival in the fortunes of the Liberal Party by the winter of 1972–3, with much talk of the need for a realignment of British politics to produce an effective 'Centre Party'. The Liberals got up to 10 per cent in the opinion polls in 1972, averaged 15 per cent in the spring of 1973 and were recording as much as 20 per cent by the autumn.

At least for the purposes of this study it is possible to discern striking similarities between the Labour government which came into power (without an overall parliamentary majority) in 1974 and Heath's government of 1970. Both were determined, although in very different ways, to break away from the consensus politics of the post-war era. Labour entered office with a series of policies more radical than any endorsed by the party since 1945. According to David Coates, 'the shift to the left in language and programme after 1970 was on a scale last seen . . . as long ago as 1931' (Coates, 1980, p. 2). Though there was a remarkable continuity of personnel from the Labour government which had lost power in June 1970 – in particular Wilson was once again prime minister – the presence of key left-wingers at the departments of Employment (Michael Foot) and Industry (Tony Benn) indicated a significant change of course. Foot's appointment was particularly interesting. The existing Shadow Employment Secretary, Reg Prentice, was regarded as unacceptable to the trade unions. 'We agreed', recalled Jack Jones of the Transport and General Workers Union, 'that Michael Foot would be the ideal choice' (J. Jones, 1986, p. 281). Yet the history of Wilson's government closely paralleled that of Heath's to the extent that the radical promise was largely frustrated. According to one left-wing critic, 'with the election [of October 1974] over, and in the face of persistent inflation, low rates of investment, heavy foreign debts and periodic currency crises, the Labour government slipped imperceptibly but steadily away from what the left of the Party had held to be the radical promise of the opposition years' (Coates, 1980, p. 11).

Labour won the two general elections of 1974 primarily on its claim that it could work successfully with the trade unions. The bitter confrontations of the period 1971–4 had re-established Labour's claim to enjoy a special relationship with the trade unions, notwithstanding the brief interlude surrounding *In Place of Strife* in 1969. Moreover, it had been the left-wing trade union leaders who had, via the block vote, provided crucial support for the adoption of Labour's new programme at the vital party conferences of the early 1970s. The repeal of the Tories' hated Industrial Relations Act was central to Labour's programme. It would not be necessary. The Social Contract would allow for a superior and more fruitful relationship with the unions. Certainly Labour proceeded to identify itself more closely with the trade union movement than had its predecessors in 1945 and 1964. Wilson's first meeting after becoming prime minister was with the General Council of the TUC. Foot quickly settled the miners' strike: at 29 per cent the settlement involved few concessions from the National Union of Mineworkers. He remained throughout a reliable champion of the workers' cause in government. 'His only policy', suggested one of Foot's civil servants, was 'to find out what the unions want' (Castle, 1980, p. 159). Some argued, with a little exaggeration, that Congress House became virtually a department of government. One opinion poll revealed the public's perception that Jack Jones had become the most powerful man in the land. This was not the case. As several commentators have pointed out, union influence on the government's economic policy was never total and declined after 1975 (Taylor, 1993, p. 243). Even so, the widespread belief was that the unions' input into the corporate state had never been greater.

Opinions on the Social Contract are, however, varied. One Treasury minister was scathing: 'To my mind the only give and take in the contract was that the government gave and the unions took' (J. Barnett, 1982, p. 49). 'The climate of the time', recalled Roy Jenkins, now a somewhat uncomfortable member of Wilson's cabinet, 'was that of ministers finding out what the TUC wanted and giving it to them' (Jenkins, 1991, p. 392). By contrast a socialist critic argued that, within a year, crude wage restraint became the centrepiece of the contract, while the government's part in terms of radical policies in the fields of industrial relations, industrial democracy, investment, housing, prices and social benefits was largely abandoned (Coates, 1980, p. 82). What seems less open to dispute is that the contract singularly failed to provide a satisfactory basis for the management of the economy. In return for the 'social wage' the unions were expected to restrain their pay demands. Within its first year inflation soared to 27 per cent, though many would now attribute this to the expansion of the money supply by the outgoing Conservative government. By June 1975 earnings had increased by an average of 26.6 per cent and weekly wages by 33 per cent. There was serious concern that the economy was out of control and in July 1975 a formal incomes policy was introduced. By October 1975 the British economy was producing less than at any time since 1970, while unemployment had passed the seasonally adjusted one million mark. Over the previous three years public expenditure had grown by almost a fifth, while output had risen by less than 2 per cent. Public spending now accounted for a massive 60 per cent of gross domestic product. Meanwhile, and even allowing for the slow-down in the world economy, Britain's rate of growth remained disappointingly slow by international standards. Between 1974 and 1979 the economy grew by only just over one per cent per annum in real terms. This compared with 2.4 per cent in Germany, 2.9 per cent in France and 4.1 per cent in Japan (Porter, 1994, p. 353).

Also central to Labour's strategy as worked out in opposition was the role of the National Enterprise Board. Its functions were to help establish and develop particular industries, extend public owner-ship into profitable manufacturing industries, and promote indus-trial democracy. The aim was to create a state holding company to establish 'a major public stake in manufacturing industry'. This would work in conjunction with a system of planning agreements linking the government to the policies of major companies. The government's Industry Bill was passed in November 1975 and by early 1976 companies which had come wholly or partly into public ownership included Ferranti, Alfred Herbert, British Leyland and Triang. But the inclusion of British Leyland in the NEB's portfolio drained the Board of much of its financial resources while ensuring, contrary to the original intention, that its role would be largely that of a rescuer of industrial lame ducks instead of the vehicle for a major shift in the ownership of British industry. Planning agree-ments also proved to be a disappointment. Only one such agreement was signed with a company in the private sector, an agreement which the company, the American motor manufacturer Chrysler, subsequently broke with impunity (Shaw, 1996, p. 125). By early 1975 Benn was already fighting a rearguard action to salvage the government's industrial strategy. Under his successor, Eric Varley, the whole policy was rapidly watered down, not least in relation to funding for Benn's favoured workers' cooperatives. Overall the emphasis of the government's industrial policy moved away from intervention and control towards the conventional ideas of exhortation and support.

Broadly speaking, the failure of Labour's leftward lurch may be explained by two factors, one domestic and one external. Despite the presence of men such as Foot and Benn – and Benn was moved to the less sensitive Energy department in June 1975 – the majority of the cabinet were of the party's right and centre, making the translation of Labour's 1973 programme into reality always somewhat problematical. Labour's constitutional structure generally allows the party leadership to reassert its authority over extra-parliamentary groupings and the parliamentary party once Labour is in government. In his heart Wilson had never been enthusiastic about the industrial strategy that had been worked out in the years of opposition. He had come to regard Benn with a mixture of suspicion and disdain. According to his press secretary, the prime minister read the Industry's Department's draft White Paper soon after coming to power. He 'said it was woolly rubbish and he would have to do it himself' (Whitehead, 1985, p. 129). Wilson was concerned by the perception that the Labour Party had moved dangerously far to the left, but he had no overall strategy for stopping or reversing this development (Ziegler, 1993, p. 419). He therefore employed those tactical political skills for which he had become renowned. He used the loss of prestige which the anti-marketeer Benn incurred following the 'yes' vote in the EEC referendum to demote him to the Department of Energy. Wilson's crucial appointment, however, was that of Denis Healey as Chancellor. A few months before Labour's election victory Healey had given a fleeting impression that he too was in the vanguard of the party's socialist advance, telling the 1973 party conference to expect 'howls of anguish' from the ranks of the rich because of Labour's tax plans. But his budget speech of November 1974 revealed him to be an orthodox Chancellor pursuing orthodox budgetary targets. Chancellor throughout the Labour government, from 1974 to 1979, Healey received the sort of abuse from Labour's left wing that is usually reserved for the most hated Tory. But he also ensured that the government remained more firmly rooted in the centre ground than might have been expected in 1974.

The external factor was perhaps even more important. As with Heath's government before it, Labour's policy options were severely circumscribed by the state of the world economy. In the face of the massive oil price increases of 1973 Healey at first decided to maintain Labour's public spending plans and to borrow to meet the deficit (J. Barnett, 1982, p. 23). Soon, however, the balance-of-payments deficit came to constrain the government at every turn. To deal with it became a prime object of the government's policy. But massive borrowing meant that foreign creditors held the whip hand over the British economy because of their ability to withdraw their loans or move out of sterling on a huge scale. As the world moved into recession, one nation after another gave up the struggle to sustain growth and reverted to deflationary policies. Short of retreating behind an eastern European style siege economy, the British government had little alternative but to follow suit.

But the world had ceased responding to a recession with the traditional Keynesian methods. The new policies of monetarism were in vogue. The control of inflation had overtaken the maintenance of full employment in the hierarchy of economic objectives. By 1975 Labour was in danger of leaving the post-war consensus behind, but not in the sense intended when the government had taken office only a year before. In a speech in his Leeds constituency in January, Denis Healey declared that wage inflation was pricing people out of jobs and that cash limits needed to be imposed on public expenditure. It was, commented Peter Jay writing in *The Times*, 'the most controversial inversion of post–1944 conventional wisdom about the management of the economy' (Morgan, 1990, p. 378). In his budget of April 1975 Healey effectively abandoned the commitment to full employment. Instead of spending his way out of recession, Healey proposed to reduce the government's deficit. He raised income tax to 35 pence in the pound and slashed spending programmes by £900 million. Jay noted that the Chancellor's basic strategy was 'to make unemployment the automatic reward for excessive pay settlements by keeping monetary creation within predetermined limits' (Pimlott, 1992, p. 661). It was an historic moment. In August it became known that the retail price index had risen by 26.9 per cent over the previous twelve months, the highest figure recorded since the war. Three months later it was announced that cash limits, as yet unfixed, would be imposed on all public expenditure.

Labour's policies also underwent an about-turn on the central foreign policy issue of continued membership of the EEC. The party's special conference in April 1975 voted by a majority of two to one for withdrawal, but when a referendum was held in June the government recommended a 'yes' vote to the proposition of staying in, and the country accepted its advice. The episode encapsulated the on-going tension between the Labour government and the Labour Party which characterized these years. Thus, by the time of his sudden resignation in April 1976, Wilson had succeeded in turning his government 'towards Europe, incomes policy and the mixed economy' and away from the fundamentalist socialism of the 1973 programme (Whitehead, 1985, p. 154).

Yet if the Labour government had returned to the centre, the Labour Party still seemed firmly orientated towards the left in a way that would be important for the increasingly polarized politics of the 1980s. After a long period in which the parliamentary party had been dominated by the right, a clear change was evident after 1974. Nearly half of the fifty-four newly-elected MPs from the February General Election joined the left-wing Tribune Group. Ian Mikardo, an old-fashioned Bevanite who had been a leading light in the Keep Left Group back in 1947, now became chairman of the parliamentary party. In 1975, while Tony Benn topped the poll in the NEC elections, Denis Healey was voted off. At the 1976 party conference both Healey and Callaghan were shouted down. Conference passed motions in favour of nationalizing the four main clearing banks and the seven largest insurance companies. The NEC document *Labour's Programme for 1976* called for the public ownership of the leading companies in all key sectors of British industry. Meanwhile some of the party's prominent right-wingers found their positions increasingly untenable. The former minister, Christopher Mayhew, had already left Labour to join the Liberals in July 1974. A year later the cabinet minister, Reg Prentice, was invited to step down as an MP by his local party's general management committee. He left the government in 1976 to sit as an independent. The party's former deputy leader, George Brown, also resigned his membership in 1976 (Paterson, 1993, p. 270). Most importantly, a disillusioned Roy Jenkins quit the House of Commons in January 1977 to take up the Presidency of the European Commission. Such developments left few in any doubt that a fundamental change was taking place in the character and identity of the British Labour Party.

The new Labour prime minister, James Callaghan, experienced a baptism of fire. The year 1976 saw the explicit and almost total abandonment of the goals with which Labour had begun its term of office. Healey's spring budget indicated that he had accepted a monetarist solution to the country's problems. In July a package of spending cuts was announced, accompanied by a rise in interest rates and a statement from the Chancellor that monetary growth should be restricted to 12 per cent in 1976–7. Such measures, however, were not sufficient to prevent a dramatic fall in the value of the pound, leading the government to seek a loan of nearly four billion dollars from the International Monetary Fund. To achieve this subvention the government was forced to accept further increases in taxation and cuts in public expenditure. The IMF took the line that large expenditure cuts were necessary to reduce the Public Sector Borrowing Requirement and restore international confidence. During the loan negotiations it became clear that the government would have to trim £2.5 billion from the PSBR over two years, sell off £500 million of BP shares and enforce a strict control over the money supply. In relation to the sale of BP shares Healey became, inadvertently, a harbinger of privatization.

The terms were harsh, some thought draconian. Symbolically, it was Anthony Crosland, one of the standard-bearers of Keynesianism and post-war social democracy, who led the resistance inside the cabinet. The IMF package was 'wrong economically and socially, destructive of what he had believed in all his life' (Benn, 1989, p. 674). But the government had little alternative and in any case, though the pressure was external, the thrust of policy was in the same direction as that upon which Healey had been engaged for nearly two years. The spending cuts of December 1976 were the fourth set that the government had enforced (Artis, Cobham and Wickham-Jones, 1992, p. 57). Phillip Whitehead comments: 'It looked to Labour activists then, and seems in memory now, like the death of Keynesian welfare socialism and the birth of monetarism, the external dictatorship of the markets and the American bankers'

(Whitehead, 1985, p. 200). It certainly represented the abandonment of the last remnants of the socialist programme upon which Labour had come to power (Pimlott, 1992, p. 724).

A speech which Callaghan delivered at the Lord Mayor's banquet in November indicated how far Labour had travelled since 1973:

> We must make a success of the mixed economy by adhering to an industrial strategy worked out and agreed by both the T.U.C. and the C.B.I., which aimed at giving absolute priority to industrial needs ahead of even our social objectives. (quoted in Coates, 1980, p. 35)

But his speech to the party conference in September, disavowing any faith in Keynesian demand management, showed how far Labour had come in the years since 1945:

> We used to think that you could just spend your way out of recession and increase employment by cutting taxes and boosting Government spending. I tell you, in all candour, that that option no longer exists, and that in so far as it ever did exist, it only worked . . . by injecting a bigger dose of inflation into the economy, followed by a higher level of unemployment as the next step. Higher inflation followed by higher unemployment . . . .. That is the history of the last twenty years. (Callaghan, 1987, p. 426)

The Labour government's real cuts in public expenditure had 'no parallel in any other period in the post-war years' (Burk and Cairncross, 1992, p. 190). But it was striking and indicative of the spending priorities of what was always, despite the bravura of 1973–4, very much a middle-of-the-road government that one key area remained exempt from the cabinet's axe. This was the Chevaline scheme to update Britain's nuclear deterrent. Escalating expenditure on this project was approved by a small group of ministers, without the knowledge of the Treasury's Chief Secretary who supposedly had responsibility for all aspects of government spending. In 1977 the government even accepted a NATO decision to increase defence spending with effect from 1979 (Shaw, 1996, p. 145).

Throughout its life the Wilson–Callaghan government enjoyed only a precarious parliamentary existence. From 1977–8 its continuation in office depended on a pact with the Liberal Party of David Steel. Despite some temporary success in controlling wage rises and inflation, which dropped to 8 per cent in the summer of 1978, the government ultimately fell, rather as Heath's had done, the victim of its own incomes strategy after the celebrated 'winter of discontent'. The proposed limit of 5 per cent on the next round of pay rises lacked the support of the TUC. As one Labour MP put it, the government 'had used up its goodwill. It had traded on the unions for four years' (Holmes, 1985a, p. 129). Ironically, a government which had placed such store on the need for co-operation with the unions came to an end amidst a wave of industrial unrest. In the ensuing general election, despite a figure of 1.3 million unemployed, it was striking that the electorate seemed to identify inflation as the key political issue. As Margaret Thatcher took office as Britain's first woman prime minister in May 1979, thirty-four years had elapsed since the end of the Second World War. Those years had been divided equally between Labour and Conservative governments. However history comes finally to judge this period, there were few in 1979, on left or right, who believed that either party had yet found the appropriate policies to deal with Britain's problems. The IMF crisis in particular had shattered what was left of the self-confidence of the old Keynesian establishment. If a consensus still existed in 1979, it was perhaps that the time was ripe for a genuinely new beginning.

5

The Consensus Overthrown, 1979–87

Mrs Thatcher made something of a virtue of her determination to break the post-war consensus. To an audience in Cardiff in April 1979 she announced:

> I am a conviction politician. The Old Testament prophets did not say 'Brothers, I want a consensus'. They said 'This is my faith. This is what I passionately believe. If you believe it too, then come with me.' (quoted in Rose, 1980, p. 4)

Two years later she dismissed the idea of consensus as 'the process of abandoning all beliefs, principles, values and policies . . . avoiding the very issues that have got to be solved merely to get people to come to an agreement on the way ahead' (quoted in Kavanagh and Morris, 1989, p. 119). Consensus was something politicians reached when they could not genuinely agree (Ingham, 1991, p. 384). The destruction of the consensus would, she hoped, one day become one of the lasting achievements for which she would be remembered. The reason for her hostility was clear. In Mrs Thatcher's mind consensus was equated with the appeasement of socialism and the progressive advance of collectivism since 1945. By it, Tories had connived in inflation and allowed the government to be dictated to by the trade unions. That process had now not simply to be stopped, but actually reversed. She therefore regarded believers in consensus politics within her own party 'as Quislings, as traitors' (H. Young, 1989, p. 223). Not surprisingly, two obviously 'socialist' elements in the consensus – the nationalized industries and trade union power – would be special objects of her government's assault.

If the consensus had enjoyed greater success during the years of its ascendancy, it would have been less vulnerable to frontal attack in 1979. But 'there is no gainsaying that the first thirty post-war years of consensus politics coincided with both a steady reduction in Britain's international standing and a relative economic decline' (Kavanagh, 1987, p. 57). As Arthur Seldon of the Institute of Economic Affairs put it in 1984: 'Sceptics [used to] say to us, in defence of collectivist policies, "Give them time. They'll work in the end." By the mid–1970s they had been saying it for thirty years and could no longer ask for more time' (quoted in Ramsden, 1996, p. 418). As has been seen, the country had achieved a lower rate of economic growth than most other industrial nations. It was a trend which one government after another had pledged itself to reverse, but without success. 'Many of the ideas and policies identified with the post-war consensus gradually came to be regarded as causes and symptoms of Britain's decline' (Kavanagh, 1987, p. 124). In absolute terms, the audit of Britain's economic performance was much less bleak. In every year from 1945 to 1973, with the exception of 1958, the British economy had grown. The result had been the most rapid rise in living standards and social welfare provision in the country's history. The most recent experience, however, had been less satisfactory. During the 1970s British unemployment had trebled, averaging well over a million for the four years up to 1979, while inflation rose twice as fast as it did in the average of the OECD (Organization for Economic Cooperation and Development) countries. Not surprisingly, there was by the end of the decade a profound feeling of pessimism about Britain's future. Richard Rose, in a book symbolically entitled *Do Parties Make a Difference?*, suggested that, whoever was in office in the 1980s, 'the problems of the British economy may become even worse than before' (Rose, 1980, p. 140).

But it was not just a set of political policies which came into disrepute during the course of the 1970s. It was also clear that the whole centre-left ideology of the post-war era had lost its intellectual ascendancy (Morgan, 1990, p. 437). The culture which had sustained it for more than a quarter of a century was in the process of disintegration. Britain's international image was one of 'accelerating decline, confusion, nervousness, decay and fratricidal battle' (Cosgrave, 1989, p. 295). 'From striking trade unionists and mass pickets to nationalists in Ireland, Scotland and Wales, there was a mounting pattern of sectional disarray amounting to lawlessness' (Morgan, 1990, p. 352). Evidence suggested that the political classes no longer inspired the confidence and respect of the ordinary citizen in the way they had once done. The circumstances in which the Heath and Callaghan governments had collapsed only encouraged this trend. Observers even began to ask whether Britain had become ungovernable.

Both the Conservative government of 1970 and its Labour successor of 1974 had, of course, been just as pledged as Mrs Thatcher to break the mould of post-war politics. Each had failed. James Callaghan warned that Mrs Thatcher's arrival presaged far more than the 'normal change of policies' associated with the election of a new government. Shortly before polling day in 1979 he confided to a policy adviser that he sensed a 'sea-change in politics' of the kind which happened every thirty years or so in British public life and which was beyond the control of a politician such as himself (Donoughue, 1987, p. 191). With the inevitable exaggeration of political rhetoric, Callaghan later concluded: 'What we are seeing today is an attempt to take us back to the nineteenth century' (quoted in Rose, 1980, p. 157). Others, however, drawing on past experience, were sceptical about the new government's ability to effect a long-term change in the direction of British politics. In April 1979 the editor of the *Sunday Telegraph* predicted that 'Whatever happens in the election is not going to make much difference. There will be neither revolution nor counter-revolution.' Any change would be measured 'in inches not miles' (quoted in Kavanagh, 1987, p. 207). If Mrs Thatcher were to succeed, momentarily, in striking out in new directions, it was widely assumed that she too, like Heath in 1972 and Callaghan in 1976, would be brought back towards the centre via an inevitable U-turn.

But the Thatcher Revolution was more closely in tune with the social, economic and intellectual mood of its time than had been the experiments of her predecessors. It is therefore necessary to say something of the emergence of the New Right in Conservative thinking.

The 1979 Conservative manifesto bore some striking similarities to that of 1970. Both, for example, stressed the invigorating power of the market economy. But Mrs Thatcher's Conservatism was much more firmly based both in economic theory and ideological vision than had been Heath's flirtation with the political right between 1965 and 1972. By about 1973 inflation had taken over from unemployment as the most pressing problem of both the British and international economies. The perceived failure of Keynesianism by the mid-1970s cleared the way for the revival of an alternative economic theory that had lain largely dormant through the consensus years. The quest for a solution to inflation gave scope for the monetarist school of economists to enjoy a new vogue of popularity. Its most celebrated exponent was the American, Milton Friedman, awarded the Nobel Prize for Economics in 1976, the two-hundredth anniversary of the publication of Adam Smith's *Wealth of Nations*, upon which much of his thinking was based.

According to Friedman and the so-called 'Chicago School', inflation can only be cured by controlling the supply of money. In other words, money, like everything else, is subject to the laws of supply and demand. If, therefore, government creates an excessive supply of money, its value will fall and inflation result. During the General Election campaign of October 1974 Friedman had insisted that there was no mystery about why the British people were suffering from the miseries of inflation. This could not be blamed upon the Labour government which had only been in power since February. The problem was simply that the Heath government had printed too much money. In Britain an important role was played by the leading economic correspondents of the *Financial Times* and *The Times* in popularizing monetarist ideas. Both Samuel Brittan and Peter Jay were disillusioned Keynesians, only too conscious that existing policies no longer offered a choice between rising prices and unemployment. Jay it was who drafted the key passage of the speech which his father-in-law, James Callaghan, delivered to the 1976 Labour party conference, in which the latter disavowed Keynesian demand management.

Also important in the intellectual origins of the New Right was the Austrian, Friedrich von Hayek. A distinguished economist himself – he was awarded the Nobel Prize in 1974 – it was Hayek's social philosophy, based on the centrality of the market and the threats to liberty posed by excessive government interference, which exercised most influence. Ironically his seminal work, *The Road to Serfdom*, had been published as long ago as 1944, just as the consensus of Keynes and Beveridge came to fruition. Its central argument was that freedom and planning could not be combined. All forms of socialism and planning ended inevitably in tyranny. It was striking that Hayek had dedicated his masterwork to 'the Socialists of all parties', but the very fact that he only achieved widespread international recognition through his Nobel Prize three decades after *The Road to Serfdom* was published indicated the extent to which his thinking had hitherto been marginalised.

The change of mood and attitude was an international phenomenon. Harold Wilson recalled a speech in 1976 by the German Social Democratic Chancellor, Helmut Schmidt: 'The Keynesian heresy had to be extirpated, and Milton Friedman at his best could not have excelled him' (Wilson, 1979, p. 237). It was noticeable that Mrs Thatcher's rise in Britain coincided with that of Ronald Reagan in the United States. Reagan entered the White House in January 1981. In Britain the impact of the change was particularly marked both because the economic problems seemed more acute than elsewhere, and because of the intense disappointment which Conservatives experienced at the fate of the Heath government – its U-turn in 1972 and the ignominy of its collapse two years later. 'Those of us who lived through those days were determined not to embark on the same tragic path', recalled Nicholas Ridley (Ridley, 1991, p. 173).

At the time, most Conservatives had accepted Heath's change of course without too much difficulty. At the Department of Education the high-spending Margaret Thatcher won the commendation of *The Guardian* for her December 1972 White Paper – 'more than half way towards a respectably socialist education policy' (Thatcher, 1995, p. 191). There were voices of dissent. Backbench critics included future ministers such as John Biffen and Jock Bruce-Gardyne. Nicholas Ridley got himself elected as chairman of the party's backbench Finance Committee in November 1972 with Bruce-Gardyne as vice-chairman. Ridley also helped form the Economic Dining Club to promote the case for monetarism and 'to anchor Enoch Powell into the Conservative Party' (Ridley, 1991, p. 20). The Selsdon Group emerged the following year to fight for those free-market policies which, according to its members, Heath had betrayed. It espoused the basic principle that 'what the public wants should be provided by the market and paid for by the public as consumers rather than tax-payers' (Ramsden, 1996, p. 363).

But most of the party's leading lights seemed happy to stand by Heath – at least until his loss of office in 1974. Enoch Powell spoke passionately of the inflationary effects of Heath's policies. In June 1973 he warned that the money supply would increase by a fifth in a single year, with inevitable inflationary consequences. But Powell lacked a sufficient following inside the party to make much of an impression, and even refused to stand for re-election as a Conservative in February 1974. Another prophet was needed. Between the two elections of 1974 Sir Keith Joseph, Social Services Secretary in the recent government and still a member of Heath's shadow cabinet, began to develop a radical, agonized and increasingly public critique of Heath's style of Conservatism.

'It was only in April 1974', Joseph later wrote, 'that I was converted to Conservatism. I had thought that I was a Conservative, but I now see that I was not really one at all.' Even by his own definition, this statement was somewhat misleading. Back in the 1960s Joseph had shown considerable interest in free-market economics and had shown signs of repudiating the interventionist policies on which the post-war consensus rested. Put in charge of social services in Heath's shadow cabinet in 1965, he had actively developed a policy of selectivity in the provision of welfare benefits. As Secretary of State for Social Services between 1970 and 1974, however, he had followed the traditional line of a minister placed at the head of a high spending department. Then, after the Conservatives' loss of office and under the influence of Alfred Sherman of the Institute of Economic Affairs, Joseph became a full and enthusiastic convert to the doctrine of monetarism, the key factor which had been missing in his intellectual make-up of the 1960s. It was Sherman, a one-time communist, who convinced him that 'Keynes is dead'. Heath turned down Joseph's request that the shadow cabinet should re-examine the party's fundamental beliefs in the field of economics but, perhaps unwisely for his own position, allowed him the latitude to use his shadow portfolio to range widely over the whole spectrum of Conservative policies. A crucial development was the setting up in March 1974 of an independent research unit, the Centre for Policy Studies, with Joseph as Chairman, Margaret Thatcher a director and Sherman 'Director of Studies' (Halcrow, 1989, p. 65). Its stated long-term goal was to change 'the whole climate of liberal-left anti-enterprise popular opinion' (Burgess and Alderman, 1990, p. 14).

A patently sincere man, for a politician sometimes embarrassingly so, Joseph developed his analysis into a wide-ranging challenge to the whole direction of Britain's economic management since the war. He was not concerned to make party political points, admitting that the new Labour government's problems with inflation were largely the consequence of Barber's profligacy in the previous administration. In a vain attempt to sustain the consensus, past Conservative governments had made progressive concessions to socialism, so that the supposed centre ground of politics had moved ever further to the left. Tories had thus allowed the rules of the political game to be set by their opponents. As Joseph later put it, 'the trouble with the middle ground is that we do not choose it. We do not shape it. It is shaped for us by the extremists. The more extreme the left, the more to the left is the middle ground. The middle ground is a will-o'-the-wisp' (quoted in Halcrow, 1989, p. 102). This was the so-called ratchet effect, making it ever harder for the Tories to get back to where they had been before. Joseph now called for a return to a free-market economy, the control of inflation by a strict monetary policy and extensive cuts in public expenditure. No sacred cow was beyond Joseph's sacrificial altar. 'Growth is welcome', he declared in an indictment of one of the chief goals of both leading parties. 'But we just do not know how to accelerate its pace. Perhaps faster growth, like happiness, should not be a prime target but only a by-product of other policies.' In a remark which is not without relevance for the argument of this book, Joseph suggested that the Conservatives' task involved 'reversing the trend' so that in future it would be Labour which would be entrapped by the ratchet effect while Conservatives set the agenda of political debate.

Perhaps his most important speech came at Preston during the election campaign of October 1974. Here he placed monetarism firmly on the political agenda as he singled out inflation, rather than unemployment, as the most important issue facing the country. Peter Jenkins comments: 'Here was Joseph seemingly abandoning the very goal [of full employment], tearing up the sacred Beveridge text' (P. Jenkins, 1987, p. 62). Ironically, Joseph was calling for a break with the accumulated inheritance of policies pursued by the Labour and Conservative front benches for more than a quarter of a century at precisely the time when his party leader was proposing a merger between the parties in the national interest. Heath made the call for a coalition government central to his campaign in the General Election of October 1974 and even promised to accept Labour's new Trade Union and Labour Relations Act despite its considerable extension of trade union rights (Ramsden, 1996, p. 414). Conscious that the Conservatives had lost a million votes to the Liberals in the February election, Heath saw no advantage in moving his party further to the right.

Joseph's chances of succeeding Heath as Conservative leader were effectively destroyed by a further speech in Birmingham in which he seemed to some to imply that mothers from lower-class backgrounds should be encouraged to have fewer children, so that they would pose less of a burden for the welfare services. It was in these circumstances that Margaret Thatcher emerged to challenge Heath for the leadership in February 1975. As Education Secretary throughout Heath's government, she had been one of the cabinet's high-spending ministers, and had not seemed particularly troubled by the U-turns of 1971–2. But it would be unfair to suggest that she emerged from nowhere to take over the mantle vacated by Joseph. In a somewhat vague sense she was regarded as a figure on the right of the party and, though her private views had not received much publicity hitherto, the evidence was there for those who wished to find it. In 1968 she had argued that consensual politics 'could be an attempt to satisfy people holding no particular views about anything', and the following year was quoted as saying that the test of the correctness of industrial policies was the market place (Ramsden, 1996, p. 443). During 1974 she had emerged as a willing recipient of Joseph's monetarist ideas and also, since the Tories lost office, as a formidable parliamentary performer in her capacity as a shadow Treasury spokesman. Anticipating her triumph in the leadership contest, Tony Benn judged that the quality of political debate would be raised 'because the Tory Party will be driven to the right and there will then be a real choice being offered to the electorate' (Benn, 1989, p. 311). But Mrs Thatcher's victory over Heath was only in part the expression of a swing to the right in the Conservative ranks. More important was a back-bench revolt against Heath as a political loser – he had lost three out of the four general elections in which he had led the party – and a man who had lost touch with his own MPs. As Hugo Young put it, 'the defenestration of Heath was essentially a personal not an ideological event' (Young, 1989, p. 96). One Tory wit spoke of 'the Peasants' Revolt'.

During the period 1975–9 the details of what became known as 'Thatcherism' were worked out. This involved the abandonment of the post-war consensus in many of its aspects and the creation of a very different socio-economic vision. This was all done very consciously. As Nigel Lawson later put it: 'Our chosen course does represent a distinct and self-conscious break from the predominantly social democratic assumptions that have hitherto underlain policy in post-war Britain' (quoted in Kavanagh, 1987, p. 13). It was much more than just picking up the ideas which Heath had abandoned in 1972. The consensus had produced a regime of high taxation, over-mighty trade unions and overmanned and inefficient industries. At the same time the welfare state had degenerated into a dependency culture in which people relied too heavily on the state provision of benefits, thereby destroying initiative and enterprise. In this way economic decline and social decadence were linked as associated evils. The New Right looked to the way in which countries such as West Germany and Japan, which made a point of emphasizing free enterprise, had done much better than Britain in the same period. Thatcherism looked therefore to the market rather than the state to allocate resources. It vehemently opposed the sort of state activities which the Butskellite consensus had taken for granted. The individual must show a sense of responsibility and a spirit of enterprise for Britain to become competitive again in relation to other countries. That enterprise would be rewarded by tax cuts to allow those who risked their capital to keep a larger share of resulting profits. This rethink went on in a favourable intellectual environment. Bodies such as the Adam Smith Institute, the Centre for Policy Studies and the Institute of Economic Affairs acted as think-tanks for the idea that only capitalism could guarantee the freedom of the individual and that the long march of collectivism had to be reversed.

Within the Conservative Party, however, Mrs Thatcher and Sir Keith had to tread warily. Most of their senior colleagues were sceptical of, and in some cases hostile to, the new ideas. The policy document, 'The Right Approach to the Economy', published in 1977, was something of a compromise. 'In framing its monetary and other policies the Government must come to *some* conclusions about the likely scope for pay increases if excess public expenditure or large scale unemployment is to be avoided; and this estimate cannot be concealed from the representatives of employers and unions whom it is consulting.' Those who wished to abandon all notion of an incomes policy and leave market forces to prevail had clearly been held in check. Tensions within the shadow cabinet were never fully resolved. At this stage of her career Mrs Thatcher's inherent caution prevailed over the instincts of a conviction politician. But it was noticeable that the party's 1979 manifesto, for the first time since the war, avoided any commitment to full employment. This was despite its effective use of the slogan 'Labour isn't working' as a commentary on existing levels of unemployment. The Conservative victory in 1979 is most properly viewed as a massive vote of no confidence in the outgoing Labour government, rather than a popular endorsement of the ideas of the New Right. The full nature of what became 'Thatcherism' was scarcely appreciated by the electorate.

As has been seen, many did not believe that Mrs Thatcher would in practice be able to give a significantly different turn to the direction of British politics. Cabinet sceptics were confident of their ability to keep the government in the traditional centre ground. James Prior, Employment Secretary in the new government, later recalled: 'I thought that we would at least be able to avoid most of the follies which new Governments tend to commit and that we wouldn't be stupidly right-wing and doctrinaire about economic policy, as we had been between 1970 and 1972' (Prior, 1986, p. 115). The majority of Mrs Thatcher's first cabinet, and especially of its most senior ministers, belonged indisputably to the One-Nation tradition of earlier Conservative governments. But the key posts in the economic ministries were held by true believers who had fully recanted the politics and policies of the consensus. Most important were Joseph at Industry and Sir Geoffrey Howe, the new Chancellor.

The historian steps at his peril into the events of the last two decades. The quests for objectivity and perspective are intrinsic to his craft and assessments of the very recent past must be recognized as hesitant and provisional. It is probably still too soon to attempt a definitive judgement on the achievements of the Thatcher years and the extent to which she succeeded in changing the course of post-war British history. Opinions at the moment are divided. Dennis Kavanagh concludes that the Conservatives' record since 1979 is one which has fallen short of the hopes of their more radical supporters, but that substantial changes have occurred 'compared with other governments since 1951' (Kavanagh, 1987, p. 244). According to Peter Riddell, the first Thatcher Government (1979–83) fell short of most of its central objectives (Riddell, 1983), but Martin Holmes credits it with changing the parameters of political and economic debate so markedly as to render impossible a return to the days of Keynesian consensus (Holmes, 1985b). The most comprehensive study of the 'Thatcher effect' concludes that the government's impact varied very considerably across the wide range of policy areas involved (Kavanagh and Seldon, 1989).

It is certainly true that, as with most governments, Mrs Thatcher's proved stronger on rhetoric than achievement. Indeed, she herself often emerged as a more cautious politician than her words tended to suggest. All successful politicians have to be prepared to be pragmatic and Mrs Thatcher was no exception. 'Anyone listening to Margaret Thatcher', writes Bruce Anderson, 'might find it incomprehensible that she had agreed to the Rhodesia/Zimbabwe settlement, the Anglo-Irish Agreement, the European Single Act and the decision to join the ERM, not to mention the steady increase in public expenditure' (Anderson, 1991, p. 293). Policy on public expenditure is the most interesting example of this contrast between rhetoric and reality. The government's goals were subtly modified as the years went by. The original policy of 1979 was to reduce expenditure in real terms. The Medium Term Financial Strategy (MTFS) was all important. Introduced in 1980, this was largely the work of the then Financial Secretary to the Treasury, Nigel Lawson. Presented as the central element in the government's approach to the economy, it represented a significant break with the past since targets for the growth in the money supply and the level of public sector borrowing had not normally been considered ends in themselves. The aim of progressively reducing government borrowing flew in the face of the conventional Keynesian assumption that it was perfectly acceptable for public sector borrowing to rise during a recession. Indeed, the MTFS formally abandoned the pretence that full employment and economic growth were in the gift of the government – an idea central to the post-war consensus – and set its sights on targets which the government believed it could control – monetary growth and borrowing (Bruce-Gardyne, 1984, p. 59; Keegan, 1989, pp. 60, 66–7). But the welfare costs of mounting unemployment and an increasingly ageing population left little scope for real overall savings. By 1984 policy was merely to contain spending in real terms. By 1986 it was to ensure that growing public expenditure should decline as a percentage of a faster growing gross domestic product. This was something which the Labour government had actually achieved in 1975–6 and 1977–8.

Policy on the control of inflation underwent similar revision. There was no spectacular U-turn, as many thought would be inevitable. Despite mounting unemployment which topped three million by January 1982, Howe's 1981 budget was a watershed. In the middle of a massive recession he eschewed Keynesian remedies and opted for further deflation. 'The most resolutely anti-Keynesian budget of modern times', it took a total of £3,500 million out of the public sector borrowing requirement (Morgan, 1990, p. 447). The government decided that 'the conquest of inflation, and not the pursuit of growth and employment . . . should be the objective of macroeconomic policy' (Lawson, 1992, pp. 414–15). Indeed, it was central to the Thatcherite argument, as Callaghan had seen in 1976, that inflation and unemployment were not alternatives but effectively cause and effect. Each time the government allowed inflation to take off, Britain's costs increased in relation to those of other countries with the result that British workers were priced out of their jobs.

Controlling inflation remained pre-eminent among the Thatcher government's priorities and probably still does under her successor, John Major. But the government seemed to abandon straightforward Freidmanite monetarism after about 1983, when Nigel Lawson succeeded Howe as Chancellor, largely because of the difficulty of finding an accurate and reliable measure of the money supply. By that time, indeed, the government was being criticized by Friedman himself for its failure to apply the monetarist remedy with sufficient consistency and rigour. Lawson formally downgraded the status of money supply targets in the government's thinking in October 1983. Thereafter Conservative Treasury ministers once again 'looked more like any other politicians, dodging and weaving through the economic thickets' (H. Young, 1989, p. 503). Perhaps significantly, the underlying rate of inflation stopped falling in the middle of the 1980s. In the later Thatcher years anti-inflationary policy focused primarily on the use of interest rates.

Indeed, with hindsight, the increasingly public dispute in the late

1980s between Lawson and Mrs Thatcher, backed by her personal economics adviser Professor Alan Walters, which culminated in Lawson's resignation in 1989, takes on the form of a battle between the pure monetarism upon which the government had first been elected and a more traditional attitude to the running of the economy. At least during his time as Chancellor, it would be difficult to describe Lawson as a strict monetarist. He came to the conclusion that inflation should be tackled on a number of fronts including currency stability, which could be achieved through membership of the European Exchange Rate Mechanism. This represented a partial return to the notion of fixed exchange rates that was anathema to the true free marketeer. Mrs Thatcher, by contrast, convinced that it was futile to try to 'buck the market', retained a simpler view of the inflationary problem. As she later put it, 'price rises were a symptom of underlying inflation, not a cause of it. Inflation was a monetary phenomenon which it would require monetary discipline to curb' (Thatcher, 1993, p. 33). At the time of her fall from power in November 1990, that particular argument seemed to have gone against the prime minister since, despite Lawson's resignation, Britain had entered the ERM in October of that year.

Yet it would be misleading to underplay the changes which have occurred since 1979 and the extent to which these changes have destroyed the fundamental assumptions of post-war politics. It was perhaps symbolic that Cuthbert Alport, a founder member of the 1950 'One Nation' group of Conservative MPs, resigned as a government whip in the House of Lords in 1984, citing his opinion that Mrs Thatcher had moved too far towards an insistence on the provision of health and welfare services through the market. Throughout her time in office Mrs Thatcher was subjected to an on-going attack – sometimes coded, sometimes overt – by disenchanted Tories who saw themselves as the representatives of that more middle-of-the-road, consensual Conservatism which had dominated the party's thinking in earlier decades. Francis Pym, dismissed from his post as Foreign Secretary after the 1983 General Election, quickly produced *The Politics of Consent*, 'a cool, rational argument in favour of "consensus"' (Morgan, 1990, p. 482).

David Butler is surely right to argue that the General Election of 1979 produced the most decisive changes of any election since the war (D. Butler, 1989, p. 114). The New Right was aware that many of its ideas were in no sense original, and this book has attempted to record some of the challenges to the consensus which preceded Mrs Thatcher's arrival on the scene. She recognized this herself. Her appointment as party chairman in 1975 of the almost forgotten Peter Thorneycroft, the Chancellor who had resigned in 1958 on the issue of sound money, was eloquent recognition of the continuities in the Thatcher Revolution. But Mrs Thatcher saw her task as to carry on where others had only pointed the way.

There is, of course, a case for pointing to 1976 rather than 1979 as the real break with the post-war consensus (Holmes, 1985a, p. 163). Counter-inflation policy was first given priority over employment under Callaghan. Monetary targets had first been set by Denis Healey. Callaghan's disavowal of Keynesian economics in his conference speech of 1976 has already been noted. Massive spending cuts were imposed by Labour, and in many respects the Conservatives' spending priorities after 1979 were not significantly different from those planned by Callaghan's outgoing government (Kavanagh, 1987, p. 229). One Marxist critic has argued that the growth of the welfare state came to an end in 1976 rather than 1979 (Gough, 1979, ch. 7). But there is an important difference: 'There is no evidence that Labour ministers ... were convinced by monetarist arguments' (Peden, 1985, p. 221). More probably they were deliberately talking the language which those from whom they wished to borrow wanted to hear. Healey later wrote of his own 'deep scepticism about all systematic economic theories' (Healey, 1990, p. 382). In any case, Labour had retained many elements of social-democratic thinking, not least its pay policy. In so far as Labour had abandoned Keynesian expansionism, this was regarded as only a temporary expedient until the economic climate improved. For Mrs Thatcher, on the other hand, there would be no going back. Certainly the Labour cabinet of 1976 which accepted the IMF's terms did not share the socio-political vision which for Conservatives such as Joseph and Mrs Thatcher was an intrinsic part of the new approach.

As has been suggested, the 'Thatcher Revolution' had an uneven impact. Part of the explanation, perhaps, lies in the fact that Mrs Thatcher was much less successful than some of her critics suggested in filling her government with men of her own way of thinking. This was only too apparent at the time of her resignation in 1990. Throughout her eleven-year premiership Mrs Thatcher's cabinet remained reflective of the Conservative Party as a whole with ministers such as Douglas Hurd, Chris Patten, Kenneth Clarke and Malcolm Rifkind promoted on their merits rather than because the prime minister regarded them as ideological soulmates. She may have wanted to know whether a particular minister was 'one of us', but she did not necessarily act upon the information received. Peter Walker remained a member of her cabinet from 1979 to 1990, before finally leaving the government of his own accord, despite the fact that he regularly, and sometimes publicly, criticized the main thrust of the government's economic policy. The extent of the 'Thatcher effect' therefore depended in part on the identity of the minister with direct responsibility for any given aspect of policy.

Policy towards industry is an area which saw a particularly marked break with the post-war consensus. The government was determined to adopt a non-interventionist approach. It was no part of a government's function to pick winners in the industrial arena or to tell industry how it should conduct its affairs. To begin with this proved to be a difficult policy to turn into practical reality. Against his better judgement, Sir Keith Joseph found himself as Industry Secretary having to pour government money into loss-making nationalized industries such as the British Steel Corporation. Over the years, however, and particularly as the economy grew during the 1980s, the change from earlier regimes became apparent. By 1989–90 the Department of Industry was spending 81 per cent less in real terms than it had done in 1979–80 (Ridley, 1991, p. 55). Direct subsidies to industry were virtually done away with. Indeed, it was widely reported that it was the ambition of Nicholas Ridley, Secretary of State for Trade and Industry from 1989 to 1990, to do himself out of a job, rather as the last Colonial Secretaries had done by granting independence to dependent territories.

During the Attlee government something like 20 per cent of the economy had been taken into state control. As has been seen, Conservative governments from Churchill to Douglas-Home kept the vast majority of nationalized industries in the public sector. The mixed economy seemed to be a permanent feature of the post-war landscape. Even the Heath government had little success in turning back the clock. Though a policy group chaired by Nicholas Ridley had recommended wholesale denationalization, Heath, more interested in efficiency than ownership, had set his face against it. Thomas Cook and Son was sold off, while the Coal Board was told to denationalize its brickworks and British Rail its hotels – 'a handful of pubs around Carlisle which Lloyd George had acquired in the First World War in an effort to curb drunkenness in Borders munitions factories' (Bruce-Gardyne, 1984, p. 79). But such tinkering around the edges has to be set against the massive rescue operations launched for Rolls Royce and Upper Clyde Shipbuilders. Nor in fact was the concept of privatization widely discussed in the period of policy planning under Mrs Thatcher, 1975–9 (Morgan, 1988, p. 34). It formed a fairly minor element in the Conservatives' 1979 manifesto. The first Thatcher government did see some significant measures of denationalization. British Aerospace was floated on the stock market in 1980 while almost half the shares in Cable and Wireless were sold in 1981. A management buyout of the National Freight Corporation took place in January 1982 and Amersham International was returned to the private sector the following month. A 51 per cent stake in Britoil was probably the most significant privatization before the 1983 General Election, though the government also reduced its holding in BP and sold out from the British Sugar Corporation completely.

After the successful sale of British Telecom in 1984 there was a significant increase of momentum. Telecom was followed by a wave of privatizations, of which the most important were the sale of the gas industry in December 1986 and of BP a year later. Water crossed over into the private sector in December 1989, with electricity following shortly after Mrs Thatcher's fall from power. Energy Secretary, Cecil Parkinson, even gave a long-term policy pledge that the government would privatize the coal mines. Little of this would have been thought possible as recently as 1979. One enthusiast has written of 'the largest transfer of property since the dissolution of the monasteries under Henry VIII, a transfer from the state to its citizens' (M. Pirie, quoted in Kavanagh, 1987, p. 221). In the process the government succeeded in creating a large number of new private share-owners and in financing tax cuts and debt repayment, though the difficulty of introducing the bracing winds of competition into what are mostly natural monopolies proved a limiting factor in any comparison between the rhetoric and the achievement of the privatization programme. The policy of returning state-owned industries to the private sector should be taken in conjunction with that on the sale of council houses. Indeed, the latter has been described as 'the most significant act of privatization carried out in the period' (Kavanagh and Seldon, 1989, p. 219). During the lifetime of the Thatcher government as a whole, housing accounted for about 40 per cent of the total proceeds of government sales. At the same time a substantial transformation was effected in the national pattern of home ownership.

Policy towards the trade unions is another area where the discontinuities after 1979 were particularly marked. As has been seen, throughout the post-war era Conservative governments as much as Labour ones took the trade union movement very seriously. Between 1945 and 1979 the TUC was regarded by all governments as the legitimate representative of the working population. During the same period its leadership believed that access to the prime minister, on any matter it thought important, was a right and not just a concession on the part of Downing Street. Even Edward Heath, despite the confrontational aspects of the Industrial Relations Act, strove mightily to establish a good relationship with union leaders and to secure TUC co-operation for his incomes policy from 1972 onwards. The New Right, however, held the trade unions as partly responsible for Britain's relatively poor industrial performance since the war. Influenced particularly by Heath's experience with the miners in 1972 and again in 1974, Mrs Thatcher did not believe that the unions had any particular claim to recognition in the corridors of power. Precisely because she accepted Milton Friedman's view that it was the volume of money in circulation rather than the level of wage settlements which determined the rate of inflation, she saw no particular need to court their support. They were 'simply the unacceptable face of corporatism, the epitome of all that was bad about the hated post-war settlement' (Taylor, 1989, p. 23). After 1979 the unions came to exercise an increasingly negligible influence over government policy. Len Murray, the General Secretary of the TUC, found himself frozen out of dialogue with the government in a way that none of his predecessors had been since before the Second World War. The era of convivial co-operation between government and unions – 'beer and sandwiches at No.10' had been the characteristic of the Wilson years – was at an end. Most importantly, of course, the unions were confronted by a government which did not look upon the maintenance of full employment as an overriding priority. In the circumstances the survival throughout the 1980s, albeit in a very much diminished form, of the NEDC – 'a symbol of a half-hearted corporatist past which had no place in a Britain which had decisively turned its back on the corporate State' – was one of the more surprising features of the Thatcher years (Lawson, 1992, p. 714).

Not only was it necessary to exclude the unions from the government's policy-making processes. The balance of power in industrial relations had to be radically changed in favour of management if British industry was to become more efficient and competitive. The Conservatives proceeded more cautiously than had Heath in 1971 and with better considered legislation. The cautious approach was particularly evident while James Prior was Employment Secretary, 1979–81. In 1981, however, Mrs Thatcher began to shape her cabinet more in her own image. Prior was transferred to the Northern Ireland Office while the more abrasive Norman Tebbit took over at Employment. Thereafter, over a period of time acts were put on to the statute book which severely limited union power in relation to secondary strike action and picketing, while introducing a more democratic and open structure into the unions' own affairs. Particularly important was the 1984 Act which made the existing legal immunity of a trade union which took industrial action dependent on the holding of a secret ballot among its members. Over the closed shop the government moved particularly warily. For the vast majority of Conservatives this was a singularly reprehensible anachronism, but the failure of the Heath government's efforts in this field imposed a policy of caution. Legislation in the early 1980s made the imposition of a closed shop more difficult, but it was not until the end of the Thatcher decade that the decisive measures were enacted. In 1988 the government made it illegal to dismiss an employee for not being a trade union member and the 1990 Employment Act prohibited employers from turning down job applicants on the grounds that they did not belong to a union (Dorey, 1991, p. 10). In a period of very high unemployment the unions proved incapable of mounting any effective opposition against the government's proposals and even the year-long miners' strike of 1984–5 was successfully resisted. The government, which had carefully prepared for such an eventuality, saw the total defeat of this particular strike as vital for the process of reducing both the reality and the perception of the power of the trade union movement. It is difficult not to believe that any previous government of the post-war era would have sought a compromise solution to the miners' dispute.

If the nationalized industries and the trade union movement offer examples of radical change effected by the Thatcher government, policies towards the welfare state and education still show the persistent strength of the post-war consensus. The New Right's case was clear enough. Britain had become trapped in a vicious circle with the welfare state swallowing up an ever higher proportion of national wealth and encouraging the citizen to look too readily to the state rather than his own initiative to provide for his needs. Increasing costs had resulted in higher taxes and accelerating wage inflation. Yet after eleven years in power Mrs Thatcher had not really succeeded in reducing the range of government responsibility for social security, health or education. For example, though the proportion of the population covered by private health insurance increased from 5 per cent in 1979 to 10 per cent in 1987, this still left Britain spending considerably less on private health insurance than any of her leading European competitors. Not surprisingly, therefore, the government's declared aim of reducing taxation, to leave people with more of their own money to spend as they wished, was only achieved in the context of income tax. Overall, tax revenues, excluding those from North Sea Oil, still amounted in the last full year of Mrs Thatcher's premiership to a higher proportion of GDP than before the government took office (Kavanagh and Seldon, 1989, p. 26). Though the Thatcher government spoke of the need for the individual to stop turning to government for a solution to all his problems, and while there was some movement towards a more selective provision of welfare benefits, the fundamental structure of the Beveridge system remained largely intact, particularly the National Health Service.

For the most part, the political costs of a more radical approach were deemed too high. Nevertheless, the NHS was seldom out of the headlines during the life-time of the Thatcher government. The argument was repeatedly put forward that the service was in crisis because it was being starved of funds. The whole ethos of the NHS could be seen as alien to the central tenets of Thatcherism. Even so, total spending increased from £7.5 billion in 1978–9 to £29 billion in 1989–90. The proportion of GDP devoted to the Health Service rose from 4.9 per cent to 5.2 per cent in the same period. But critics claimed that this was inadequate, granted an ageing population and the ever advancing (and ever more expensive) technology available in the provision of health care. The government's early reforms were largely concerned with the management of the service, though there were also some moves to change the status of the patient to that of a consumer. In September 1983 health authorities were required to put hospital cleaning, catering and laundry services out to competitive tendering. This, and the restrictions placed on the freedom of a GP to prescribe whatever drugs he wished, were more important in symbolic than financial terms. An attempt was being made to show that 'even the NHS could not claim automatic or unlimited freedom to use public resources as it saw fit; taxpayers who had supplied its funds had a right to demand that their money not be wasted' (Letwin, 1992, p. 215).

Not until Mrs Thatcher's third term in office was the NHS subjected to a more radical review. A White Paper published in 1988 focused on the idea of creating an internal market within the NHS. This introduced the notion that a doctor should be able to buy the best available hospital service for his patient, with the required funding 'following the patient'. It was 'an attempt to secure some of the benefits of privatization within a nationalized health service' (Letwin, 1992, p. 218). GPs who so wished were now able to become budget holders, responsible for the management of their own funds, while the proposal to allow hospitals to become self-managing trusts was designed to restore to them some of their pre-NHS independence. These were among the most significant changes introduced into the Health Service since its foundation. Even so, they fell some way short of what many on the radical right were hoping for. Part of the problem was that the electorate has proved far more attached to this aspect of the post-war consensus than to many others, and for some years the government was anxious to reiterate that the NHS was 'safe in its hands'. Indeed, opinion polls suggested that, notwithstanding her three successive general election victories, Mrs Thatcher was less than successful in converting the electorate to the underlying values upon which her political philosophy was based. The public 'remained wedded to the collectivist, welfare ethic of social democracy' (Kavanagh and Seldon, 1989, p. 243).

Broadly speaking, the same picture emerges in the field of education, at least during Mrs Thatcher's first two terms. This was despite a widespread feeling, by no means restricted to the Conservative Party, that the system designed by the 1944 Education Act was far from satisfactory, particularly in terms of what it was doing for the academically less able pupil. Indeed, it was James Callaghan in his 1976 Ruskin speech who had initiated not only the 'great debate' on educational standards but also the breakdown of the post-war consensus in this field. Yet under Mrs Thatcher the comprehensive restructuring of the 1960s and 1970s remained essentially intact and the government drew back from the idea of a consumer-orientated system based on educational vouchers. The main argument in favour of vouchers was that they would enable parents to opt for schools of their own choice rather than be restricted by the catchment area in which they happened to live. The bracing winds of the market would then be introduced for the first time into the education system so that schools would prosper or decline depending on their capacity to attract pupils. Parents would also be able to top up their vouchers if they wished to do so to enable their children to go to schools charging higher fees than the voucher's value. In this way, it was hoped, a voucher scheme would make independent schools accessible to a wider section of the population than before (Letwin, 1992, p. 238). Yet ironically it was Sir Keith Joseph, Education Secretary from 1981 to 1986 and certainly a 'true believer' in Thatcherism, who reluctantly concluded that vouchers, despite their attractiveness on intellectual grounds, involved political risks which he was not prepared to take (Halcrow, 1989, pp. 175–6). Only on the periphery did the advocates of vouchers enjoy any success. In March 1990, Michael Howard, the Employment Secretary, announced that the Youth Training Scheme would be replaced by vouchers for sixteen-year-old school leavers to enable them to buy training of their own choice (Letwin, 1992, p. 254). In general, while the government's desire in the field of education to increase parental choice was clearly proclaimed, the means by which this would be accomplished was less apparent.

Overall Joseph's long tenure of the Education ministry produced fewer fundamental reforms than might have been expected, though the introduction of the GCSE examination in 1986 was a noteworthy exception. On occasions Joseph's radicalism was restrained by his colleagues as, for example, in his failure to persuade the cabinet to replace student grants with loans. In 1984, despite a parliamentary majority of 140 seats, the government, in the face of a back-bench rebellion, had to withdraw a scheme which would have required better-off parents to contribute to students' tuition fees (Halcrow, 1989, pp. 181–2). At least until 1986, concludes one authority, the agenda of educational policy initiated by Callaghan was 'not essentially altered by the advent of the Conservative Administration in 1979' (Kavanagh and Seldon, 1989, p. 183).

As in the case of the NHS the most radical approach to education was taken during the Thatcher government's third term in office, and by an Education Secretary, Kenneth Baker, not originally thought to be close to the prime minister in ideological terms. The Education Reform Act of 1988 was certainly the most important piece of education legislation since 1944. It allowed schools to manage their own budgets and to accept as many pupils as they could house. It also permitted those schools that so wished to opt out of the control of Local Education Authorities and move over to direct funding by the government. And it allowed for the establishment of City Technology Colleges. This last provision was indicative of the government's concern that the existing school curriculum, which still owed much to the ideas and priorities of Victorian England, might not be best suited to the demands of an industrial society in the last years of the twentieth century. In similar vein, and partly in reaction to what were seen as the left-wing inclinations of the educational establishment, the government announced plans for a National Curriculum to ensure that all pupils left school with a basic grounding of knowledge. Attempts were also made to introduce the spirit of the 'enterprise culture' into higher education. The University Grants Committee was replaced by the Universities Funding Council The government was 'concerned to see that the UFC's arrangements for making funds available to universities properly reward success in developing cooperation with and meeting the needs of industry and commerce' (Letwin, 1992, p. 266).

In education as in health, therefore, the landscape looked considerably different after eleven years of Mrs Thatcher's government, yet in both cases radicalism had been mixed with caution, ideological conviction with political practicalities, much to the disappointment of many spokesmen of the 'New Right'. Mrs Thatcher's 'failures – the continuing growth of welfarism, the high cost/low productivity poor quality problems in the NHS and education – are in the areas where she was least radical or waited too long to begin her reforms' (Tebbit, 1991, p. 34). At the end of the day, perhaps the most striking fact is that in 1990, as in 1979 and 1945, health, education and social security were all still seen as proper areas of state responsibility.

Just as the creation of the post-war consensus required *both* parties to move towards a common centre ground, so too its destruction is best understood in terms of *both* parties retreating from this point of convergence. The emergence of a New Right within the Tory Party was matched by the renaissance of the left in Labour's ranks. By 1979 both were ready to condemn the consensus and see within it the seeds of Britain's decline. Both would have agreed that whichever party had been nominally in office since 1945, in practice social democracy had been in power. Thereafter, of course, their analyses diverged. While the Right believed that Britain had been brought to her knees by a stultifying collectivism, the Left discerned a crisis, possibly terminal, of the whole capitalist system. As the Right's analysis was strengthened by the experience of the Heath government, the Left drew equally compelling evidence from the Wilson–Callaghan years. Socialism and the class struggle had been betrayed while Labour governments sought to prop up the failing edifice of capitalism. The familiar cry was heard that Labour had lost the 1979 General Election because it had alienated the electorate by betraying its socialist principles. The experience of the 1976 IMF crisis and the consequent abandonment by Labour ministers of the party's traditional commitment to full employment was grist to the Left's mill (Jefferys, 1993, p. 98). Suddenly Aneurin Bevan's criticisms of the consensus, voiced back in 1944, assumed a new relevance. The Crosland vision of how to achieve a socialist society had now to be jettisoned. As in the early 1970s, Tony Benn was the most important figure in Labour's swing to the left. In many ways he was Mrs Thatcher's 'symbiotic opposite' (H. Young, 1989, p. 26). According to Peter Jenkins, Thatcher and Benn 'formed unholy alliance to dance on the grave of John Maynard Keynes' (P. Jenkins, 1987, p. 51). Kenneth Morgan made the same point slightly differently: 'it was Marx versus Adam Smith, a hundred and twenty years on' (Morgan, 1990, p. 393).

So traumatic was the experience of the last months of Callaghan's government, with Labour locked in conflict with its supposed comrades in the trade union movement, that it was not difficult to move the party rapidly to the left, with the annual conference and the National Executive Committee (NEC) achieving unprecedented power over the direction of policy. Tension was heightened by the fact that a secret draft prepared under Prime Minister Callaghan's instructions had replaced the more left-wing manifesto drafted at Transport House. The time was now ripe for a truly socialist strategy. In May 1980 the Rank and File Mobilising Committee was set up to co-ordinate the activities of all those who sought a fundamental change of direction. In June the party's own Commission of Inquiry endorsed the idea of the mandatory re-selection of MPs together with the setting up of an electoral college to choose the party leader. The right interpreted these moves, fairly enough, as designed to place Labour MPs at the beck and call of left-wing constituency and union activists (Bradley, 1981, p. 76). The election later that year, but under the old rules, of the veteran left-winger, Michael Foot, to succeed Callaghan as party leader was a sign of the times. This development presaged a fundamental split within the uneasy coalition of interests which made up the Labour Party. Had the leadership gone to Denis Healey, the party's social democrats might have been prepared to argue their case from within the movement. As it was, many now began to consider the option of leaving Labour altogether. Indeed, there is evidence that a few right-wing Labour MPs actually voted for Foot to help justify their later defection – by creating a leadership which the right could not in the long-term tolerate (Daly, 1993, p. 296).

At the party's annual conference commitments were made to an 'alternative economic strategy', including more public ownership, a reflation of the economy, selective import controls and a thirty-five hour week with no reduction in pay. The following January a special party conference agreed, against even Foot's wishes, to the creation of an electoral college for subsequent leadership elections in which the largest vote would be given to the trade unions (40 per cent) with the Parliamentary Labour Party and the constituency parties each receiving 30 per cent. Foot was also embarrassed by the selection of far-left parliamentary candidates such as Pat Wall and Peter Tatchell and by the evident advance of revolutionary Marxist groups within the party's ranks.

For some time the left had been making steady progress within the Labour movement at the grass-roots constituency level. Here a type of militant party activist had risen to prominence, whose politics had little in common with those of the average Labour voter – or even with the Labour Party of Attlee, Gaitskell and Wilson. The Labour Party in the localities 'seemed to be turning into an alienated and irreconcilable cabal of full-time revolutionaries' (Morgan, 1990, p. 390). The party leadership had chosen largely to ignore what many saw as a scarcely concealed form of entryism into Labour's ranks by people whose adherence to the traditions of democratic socialism was open to grave question. The Underhill Report on 'Entryist Activities', dealing with groups such as the avowedly Marxist, Militant Tendency, had been submitted to the NEC in November 1975 but was effectively suppressed (Bradley, 1981, p. 58). But the experience of Labour politics in cities such as Liverpool stood as an indication of the direction in which the party might now head.

All of this proved extremely distasteful to those on the party's moderate right who saw themselves as the direct descendants of a line which went back through Gaitskell to Attlee. As one right-winger put it in 1980, 'Labour's leaders no longer look for inspiration to social democracy. Nor are their guiding principles drawn from the early English utopian, Christian, Owenite tradition. What is left? Put starkly, a British version of the West European communist tradition' (Haseler, 1980, p. 73). In his Dimbleby lecture in November 1979 the party's former deputy leader, Roy Jenkins, had already called for a strengthening of the 'radical centre' in order to break the constricting rigidity of the existing party system. Jenkins believed that a life and death struggle for the party's soul was taking place and, more importantly, that this struggle was, in effect, already lost. As he later recalled, 'the constitutional disputes which were currently raging . . . about who should elect the leader, who should write the manifesto and how easily a small caucus could get rid of an MP, were not minor organisational points but part of a continuing left-right ideological battle which had crossed the divide from constructive tension and made internecine warfare the principal purpose of the party's life' (R. Jenkins, 1991, p. 518). In such circumstances Jenkins, with the support of former Labour cabinet ministers, David Owen, Shirley Williams and William Rodgers, the so-called 'Gang of Four', set up the Social Democratic Party in March 1981. Eventually, two dozen other

Labour MPs and one Tory also joined up. It was the worst split in the Labour Party's history since the traumatic events of 1931.

The new party presented itself as a radical departure in British politics. Especially once it had formed an alliance with the Liberals, the notion of 'breaking the mould' of the existing two-party structure was widely trumpeted. Yet in many ways the SDP was an extremely conservative body, harking back to the consensual politics of the 1940s, 1950s and 1960s. According to Kenneth Morgan, it was 'a mood rather than a movement, a transient phenomenon with shallow roots in the constituencies' (Morgan, 1990, p. 464). If so, it was a mood which certainly captured the popular imagination, however briefly. An opinion poll in January 1980 found that as many as 60 per cent of the population believed that the Labour Party had moved too far to the left and that 46 per cent believed that the Conservatives had moved too far to the right. With Labour in a state of internal disarray and the Conservatives deeply unpopular in the light of rapidly mounting unemployment figures, the SDP seemed for a moment to be a serious contender for political power. Michael Foot secured the dubious distinction of being seen as both too extreme and yet ineffectual; Margaret Thatcher was regarded as strident and uncaring. Some spectacular by-election successes were achieved and one Gallup poll put support for the SDP–Liberal Alliance at a staggering 55 per cent. The SDP argued that Britain needed 'a reformed and liberated political system without the pointless conflict, the dogma, the violent lurches of policy and the class antagonisms that the two old parties have fostered'. To secure Britain's livelihood in the 1990s, what was needed was a 'consistent economic strategy in the eighties, one that is not disrupted every few years by a political upheaval' (Bradley, 1981, pp. 121–2). Though these sentiments may have captured the mood of 1981, they scarcely, as this book has shown, provided an accurate commentary on the course of British politics since the end of the Second World War.

On the basis of his support among constituency activists Tony Benn reached new heights of influence within Labour's ranks, culminating in his narrow defeat by Denis Healey in the election for the party's deputy leadership in September 1981. With little difficulty Labour abandoned many of the policies which had been pursued by its own government. In contrast to the New Right, Labour's departure from the consensus affected its attitude to foreign and defence policy, as well as economic matters. By 1981, in addition to massive increases in public expenditure and public ownership, and the effective adoption of the Left's 'Alternative Economic Strategy', which the Labour cabinet had successfully resisted when in government, the party conference endorsed unilateral nuclear disarmament, withdrawal from the EEC and the closure of American nuclear bases in Britain. Even the national constitution, an unspoken assumption of the consensus, seemed under threat as Labour pledged itself to abolish the House of Lords. Not surprisingly, David Butler concludes that the 1983 election 'offered the widest choice of any post-war contest' (D. Butler, 1989, p. 114). Labour's 1983 manifesto promised a massive reflation of the economy to restore full employment and refurbish the public services. Exchange controls would be restored and selective import controls introduced. As this would be in breach of the Treaty of Rome, it was convenient that Labour also promised to withdraw from the EEC. To the delight of the Left, Labour committed itself to a non-nuclear defence policy. All privatized industries were to be renationalized 'with compensation of no more than that received when the assets were denationalized'. A so-called National Economic Assessment would ensure a return to economic planning and schemes of industrial democracy (Shaw, 1996, p. 166). It was, quipped one insider, 'the longest suicide note in history'.

With the opposition vote badly split between Labour and the SDP–Liberal Alliance, Mrs Thatcher secured an overwhelming victory with a majority of 144 seats in the new parliament, even though the Conservatives' percentage of the popular vote was slightly down on 1979. By this time the Conservatives, and Mrs Thatcher in particular, were greatly strengthened by victory in the Falklands War and by signs that the economy was beginning to turn around. Even so, the unemployment total was continuing to rise remorselessly and did not peak until April 1985 at what would once have been regarded as the politically catastrophic figure of 3.2 million. This in itself was an interesting commentary on the change in attitudes that had taken place since the years of the consensus.

With hindsight it is clear that Benn's challenge for the deputy leadership represented the high-water mark in the Left's advance within the Labour Party. The years that followed were characterized by a split within the Left, caused in part by the failure of some key left-wingers to cast their votes for Benn. The division into so-called Hard and Soft Left factions resulted in considerable personal animosity and public abuse and allowed the Right (or what remained of it) to reassert its traditional domination of the shadow cabinet, often in alliance with the Soft Left (Seyd, 1987, p. 165). The election of Neil Kinnock from the latter group as party leader in succession to Foot in the wake of the 1983 electoral débâcle was a further significant development. Benn had lost his parliamentary seat at the election and was therefore not able to stand in opposition to Kinnock. As Labour now embarked upon a slow but definite movement back towards the political centre, the inevitable result was that the two main parties began, at first imperceptibly, to come together once more.

By 1985 Kinnock had begun to realize that Labour would be unelectable if it stood by many of the policies which had been presented to the electorate in 1983. As after 1959, there was considerable discussion of the proposition that Labour was in irreversible decline. Opinion polls showed that many aspects of the Conservative legislative programme were very popular with the electorate. Labour's existing policies over the sale of council houses and withdrawal from the EEC were abandoned without too much difficulty, but on other issues Kinnock had to move with caution (Shaw, 1996, p. 176). The Tories' trade union reforms were a case in point granted the close relationship which had existed between Labour and the unions since its earliest days. No Labour leader was likely to forget the way in which Wilson had burnt his fingers over the question of trade union legislation in 1969. But it was a sign of changing times that Kinnock managed partially to distance himself from the miners' leader, Arthur Scargill, during the national coal strike in 1984–5. Eventually a compromise was reached in 1986 whereby, though much of the existing legal framework would be repealed by a future Labour government, the obligation for unions to hold strike ballots and elections for leading union officials would be reaffirmed. *The Times* had already described Labour's new programme as 'Gaitskellism from the left of centre' (Morgan, 1987, p. 338). Meanwhile even Labour's sacred goal of public ownership was watered down with nationalization giving way to the more restricted concept of 'social ownership'. With Kinnock personally deeply committed to unilateralism, defence remained a more difficult area for policy revision and one which the Conservatives were still able to exploit to good effect. All this scarcely amounted to an acceptance of the Thatcherite Revolution, but it was a step in that direction.

Kinnock also proved willing to tackle the question of extremism within Labour's own ranks, a problem to which his immediate predecessors had tended to turn a blind eye with, many believed, catastrophic consequences. At the 1985 party conference he launched a passionate attack on the Militant Tendency with the example of the Liverpool City Council particularly in his sights. In a memorable speech he attacked 'the grotesque chaos' of the city's Labour councillors hiring taxis to deliver redundancy notices to their own workers. The complete extirpation of groups such as Militant was, however, a long-term process and, by the time of the 1987 General Election Kinnock had not yet convinced the electorate that he had been sufficiently effective. Between 1983 and 1987 Labour's policy changes had been 'significant' but 'not substantial'. Its 1987 election manifesto was 'full of compromise and ambiguity' (Smith, 1992, pp. 9–10). In that election the Labour Party made only a partial recovery. Mrs Thatcher and the Conservatives were rewarded for low inflation, falling unemployment and widespread prosperity. They held on to their share of the popular vote and still had an overall parliamentary majority of 102. Labour's one consolation was that it managed to pull significantly ahead of the SDP–Liberal Alliance, a sign in part that it had largely abandoned its 1983 extremism. Even so, voters were still in no doubt that the Labour and Conservative Parties offered them a genuine set of policy alternatives. Faced with this choice they had given Mrs Thatcher a renewed endorsement.

6

Towards a New Consensus, 1987–96

The most striking event in British politics in the 1990s to date has been the overthrow of Mrs Thatcher – by her own party – as Conservative leader in November 1990. The reasons for the removal of the longest serving and electorally most successful prime minister of the twentieth century lie largely outside the scope of this book. The discussion here must focus upon the effect which the replacement of Mrs Thatcher by John Major has had upon the nature of the party political debate. Many had always claimed that it was Mrs Thatcher herself who had, almost single-handedly, taken the Conservative Party away from the consensual paths of Macmillan and Butler and into dangerous new areas which had little real connection with the long tradition and history of Conservatism. She was an aberration; her impact would last no longer than her own premiership. Not surprisingly, Edward Heath, still smarting from his own loss of the party leadership to Mrs Thatcher, was one of those who subscribed to this view and who therefore welcomed the change which took place in 1990. The new prime minister, Heath asserted, was 'sending a refreshing breeze through the Conservative party. At last we are beginning to shed the albatrosses that have weighed us down over the last few years' (Campbell, 1993, p. 794). Certainly those MPs who supported Michael Heseltine when he challenged Mrs Thatcher for the party leadership did so not because they wanted to take the Conservative Party further to the right, but because they believed the time had come to move the party back towards the centre ground of British politics. Prominent Heseltine campaigners such as Peter Temple-Morris and Julian Critchley were well known as being on the left of the Tory spectrum. Mrs Thatcher herself seemed to confirm this analysis when she castigated Heseltine's declared support for a more active industrial policy as 'more akin to some of the Labour party's policies: intervention, corporatism, everything that dragged us down' (Campbell, 1993, p. 787). Her own most loyal supporters, by contrast, were to be found in the aptly named 'No Turning Back' group of Conservative MPs.

In the event, of course, it was not Heseltine but John Major who emerged as the new Conservative leader and occupant of 10 Downing Street. Even after six years as prime minister, however, it remains difficult to assess what Major's impact upon the Conservative Party has been. Indeed, one of the persistent themes of his many critics has been that he seems to have little vision (at least compared with his predecessor) of where he wants to take his party and country. Many of his policy initiatives such as the Citizen's Charter have been dismissed as little more than gimmicks. Few would feel confident in assessing the identity of 'Majorism'; defining Thatcherism posed few difficulties. That ambiguity was present from the outset of John Major's premiership. He arrived at this position 'admirably unburdened by a philosophical past' (Anderson, 1991, p. 296). During his early ministerial career he was known to enjoy Mrs Thatcher's patronage, but had not been over-identified with any particular party faction. On the one hand, the Conservatives seemed to have chosen a leader who was the very antithesis of Mrs Thatcher, certainly as regards style and image. Major gave every appearance of being easy-going, moderate and compromising – descriptions which it would have been difficult to apply to his predecessor. He was elected too as the candidate most likely to be able to heal the wounds in the party's ranks which had become particularly evident during the last months of the Thatcher premiership. On the other hand, however, Major *was* the chosen candidate of the party's right-wing, securing the enthusiastic endorsement of Mrs Thatcher herself and being perceived by his fellow Conservative MPs as more likely than either of his opponents in the leadership ballot, Douglas Hurd and Michael Heseltine, to carry forward his predecessor's torch. To this extent the party had 'deliberately passed up the opportunity to choose a different ideological direction' (Kavanagh and Seldon, 1994, p. 4). The majority of the parliamentary party thus seemed to want to continue along the same paths as before, but without the stridency which many disliked in Mrs Thatcher. It was, as Kenneth Clarke put it, 'Thatcherism with a human face'.

But this element of ambiguity did not end with John Major's election as party leader. Indeed, it has tended to intensify since the General Election of 1992. Confronted by a narrow and ever diminishing parliamentary majority, Major has found it necessary to conduct a political balancing act between the various strands of Conservative thought, most of his moves having more to do with party tactics than political conviction. Early prime ministerial pronouncements seemed to indicate a distinct change of direction, though these may have had more to do with an understandable desire to stamp his own mark upon the government than any deep-seated policy differences with Mrs Thatcher. Major spoke of his desire to create a classless society and placed an improvement in public services, especially the state education system, the NHS and public transport, high on his agenda (Campbell, 1993, p. 794). This seemed to chime in with a marked change in the public mood. There was much discussion of the idea that the 1990s would prove to be more caring and compassionate than the previous decade. After a period in which 'the state was in disrepute, accused of interfering too much in people's lives', the complaint now was 'of the state's neglect, its failure to undertake the tasks which are properly its' (Peter Jenkins quoted in Campbell, 1993, p. 776).

Michael Heseltine, restored to the Department of the Environment, rapidly did away with the Community Charge, a symbolic step since this was an innovation with which Mrs Thatcher had been personally closely associated and which had played an important part in her growing unpopularity in 1989–90. But the sharpest contrast with the recent past related to policy towards the European Community, the issue which had been the immediate cause of Mrs Thatcher's fall and over which she had lost much personal support within her own cabinet, especially that of Sir Geoffrey Howe. Mrs Thatcher's relationship with the European Community had never been easy. But in her steadfast opposition to further European integration she had found herself increasingly isolated among Britain's European partners. By contrast, in a speech in Bonn in March 1991, John Major declared that Britain intended to be 'at the very heart of Europe'. During his first two years as prime minister, Major set out to change the approach (and particularly the personal chemistry) of Britain's relations with the other members of the European Community. In particular, he struck up a working relationship with Chancellor Kohl of Germany. Europhiles such as Ted Heath rejoiced that the right-wing nationalism which they attributed to Mrs Thatcher had now been extinguished.

Opinion surveys after 1990 showed that the voters saw far fewer differences between the parties than they had sensed in the 1980s and that they regarded both as moderate rather than extreme (Kavanagh and Seldon, 1994, p. 149). This, however, may tell us more about what was happening to the Labour Party than be proof of any significant change of direction by the new Conservative government. It may also provide an interesting reflection on the change in the electorate's perception of what is 'moderate' after a decade of substantial change. Even so, writing in 1995, Mrs Thatcher herself seemed to confirm that the Conservative Party of her successor had begun to drift back to the central ground of British politics. She wrote now of her 'misgivings about some Government policies' and of her need to place 'greater hope in those outside Government who still carried on the battle of ideas' (Thatcher, 1995, pp. 467–8). But her principal concerns related to Major's policy on Europe and in particular his readiness to sign the Treaty of Maastricht in 1991 – 'I was not prepared for the speed with which the position I had adopted would be entirely reversed' (Thatcher, 1995, p. 475). In key areas of policy, however, there is a good argument to suggest that, notwithstanding a softening of presentation, the Major government's overriding characteristic has been one of continuity with the Thatcher years. Even allowing for a less abrasive approach, Major's policies were always likely to appear less radical than his predecessor's precisely because so many of the key intellectual battles of the 1980s – the primacy of the market, the overriding importance of the fight against inflation, the outdatedness of nationalization and the corporate state – had already been won.

In the fields of privatization and trade union reform there is clear evidence that the Major government has attempted to continue the policies of Margaret Thatcher. Indeed, by returning British Rail to the private sector, and in at least attempting to do the same to the Post Office, Major extended a key Thatcherite policy into areas from which his predecessor had drawn back. Even Nicholas Ridley, in many ways the high priest of privatization, had concluded that the railways were not a suitable candidate for private ownership. As regards industrial relations policy, 'Mr Major has proved to be less combative and more conciliatory at least in the style of his presentation of labour market strategy, but to a very large extent there has been a strong continuity of purpose and action from the years of Margaret Thatcher' (Kavanagh and Seldon, 1994, p. 246). The Trade Union Reform and Employment Rights Act of 1993 imposed further restrictions on the ability of trade unions to call strikes. That same year the government decided to abolish the twenty-six statutory Wages Councils which had hitherto laid down minimum wage rates for 2.5 million low-paid workers. The TUC enjoyed no appreciable increase in influence under John Major. Indeed, it was the latter's government which in December 1992 finally wound up the NEDC, a body which had managed, against the odds, to survive the Thatcher decade. Perhaps most significantly, the government has placed great store by its negotiation of an 'opt-out' from the social chapter of the Maastricht Treaty of December 1991, arguing that this would impose unacceptable costs on British industry and damage its competitiveness.

In the field of education the Thatcherite revolution had, as has been seen, only really got under way in the late 1980s. But the impetus of those reforms has been maintained under John Major. It was he, indeed, who finally combined the departments of Education and Employment under a single Secretary of State, Mrs

Gillian Shepherd, thereby emphasizing the government's perception that education must serve the industrial and commercial needs of the country as a whole. Similar trends may be observed in the Health Service where, in line with initiatives launched by the Thatcher government, the great majority of hospitals had become self-governing trusts by 1994. As Secretary of State for Social Security, Peter Lilley, a convinced Thatcherite, has presided over a fundamental, long-term review of social policy, based on the proposition that social security spending will soon impose an insupportable burden on the national economy and calling into question the universality and comprehensive nature of the whole Beveridge system. Even the ill-fated 'back to basics' campaign, launched by the prime minister at the 1993 party conference, was widely seen as a shift to the right and was welcomed by Lady Thatcher herself as indicating that Thatcherism was 'alive and well' (Kavanagh and Seldon, 1994, p. 355).

But it is obviously in the management of the economy that the credentials of the Major government must ultimately be assessed. Like its predecessor, this government has placed the conquest of inflation as its primary economic objective. 'First and foremost', Major declared in one of his first speeches as prime minister, 'I loathe inflation' (Anderson, 1991, p. 294). In this respect, at least, the government has achieved considerable success, helped in part by the elevation of the Bank of England and its Governor to something approaching the status of guardians of monetary rectitude already enjoyed by the German Bundesbank and the American Federal Reserve. Continuity with the Thatcher years has been particularly clear since Britain's undignified exit from the Exchange Rate Mechanism in September 1992, even though that event did little for the prime minister's reputation or that of his government for economic competence. Leaving the ERM seemed to many to provide belated justification for Mrs Thatcher's dictum that governments cannot 'buck the market' by trying artificially to control the value of their currency. The general improvement in the economy since 1992, and in particular the fact that a floating pound has not led to a resurgence of inflation, would make any return to the ERM or a comparable successor body difficult to contemplate.

Meanwhile, with priority given to controlling inflation, any progress in reducing the high levels of unemployment which resulted from the recession of the early 1990s has been left largely dependent on the slow overall improvement of the economy. Few now speak of the virtues of 'reflation' to 'create jobs'. Strikingly, it was Major's first Chancellor of the Exchequer, Norman Lamont, who took the first steps towards the abolition of mortgage interest tax relief – a step from which Mrs Thatcher had always recoiled, despite her theoretical opposition to subsidies and other distortions of the market. In addition, the government maintains its long-term commitment to the reduction of income tax 'when economic circumstances permit', while there has been no return to the industrial policies of the 1960s and 1970s. Michael Heseltine, appointed to the Department of Trade and Industry after the 1992 General Election, proved less inclined to intervene in the free running of the market economy than some of his pronouncements during his back-bench exile from 1986 to 1990 had led one to expect.

Even policy towards Europe, the issue where John Major made a particular point of his determination to chart a fresh course, shows considerable evidence of continuity with the Thatcher years. Mrs Thatcher's criticisms may have more to do with a belated appreciation that she herself, in accepting the Single European Act of 1986, had conceded far more to the cause of European federalism than she realized at the time, than with a belief that the present government has embarked upon a distinctively different policy. Since 1990 the balance of the parliamentary Conservative Party has moved decisively towards a Eurosceptic position – precisely that outlook for which Mrs Thatcher was widely criticized before her resignation. Confronting a precarious parliamentary majority, Major has found it necessary to take account of this movement of opinion. Even a minister such as the Foreign Secretary, Malcolm Rifkind, once thought of as a Euro-enthusiast, has also found it necessary to modify his stance. In the spring of 1996, faced by an impasse over the banning of trade in British beef, Major initiated a policy of non-cooperation with Britain's European partners. Sir Michael Butler, the former British ambassador to the European

Community, contrasted this with what he believed would have been Mrs Thatcher's more cautious and diplomatic approach! As opinion in Britain moves against the idea of a single European currency, it becomes difficult to see how a Conservative government could take the country into monetary union without catastrophic consequences for party unity. Far from placing Britain at the heart of Europe, John Major's government seems, at the time of writing, as isolated within the European Union as Mrs Thatcher's ever was.

If, therefore, the government of John Major has shown no significant change of overall direction from that of Margaret Thatcher, it is to the Labour Party that we must now return to assess whether the gap between the parties is as wide in the 1990s as it was during the 1980s, or whether there are signs of the parties coming together and thus forming a new consensus. After the General Election defeat of 1987 Neil Kinnock sanctioned the party's first major policy review since the 1950s. Seven policy groups were set up to rethink Labour's approach to domestic and international affairs, with the clear aim of getting rid of those policies which were making Labour unelectable. The results were startling. Any residual proposals to extend public ownership soon disappeared. The 1989 policy statement, *Meet the Challenge, Make the Change*, committed a future Labour government to work through a successful market. It was 'the least socialist policy statement ever to be published by the party' (Crewe, 1990, p. 5). State intervention would now be limited to specific areas such as industrial training where the market was perceived to be failing. 'In our view, the economic role of modern government is to help make the market system work properly where it can, will and should – and to replace it where it can't, won't or shouldn't.' This was a long way from the socialist state still theoretically envisaged in Clause IV of the party's constitution. The change of tone was particularly apparent after the appointment of Gordon Brown as Shadow Industry Secretary in October 1989. In effect the party had 'come to terms with the irreversibility of many Thatcherite reforms by recognizing that the market economy should be regarded as innocent until found guilty, rather than vice-versa' (Jefferys, 1993, p. 122). In 1990 Labour's *Looking to the Future* declared that only the water industry, among those enterprises which had been privatized by Mrs Thatcher's governments, was to be returned to the public sector. Two years later even this commitment had been dropped, with the party settling now merely for 'public control'. It also became clear that a future Labour government would not seek to restore the steeply progressive rates of income tax which had existed before 1979. As a result, any future expansion of the public services would be dependent on Labour using the proceeds of economic growth.

As regards industrial relations legislation, Labour had by 1990 moved to an acceptance of much of the legal framework constructed by the Conservatives. This included the ban on the closed shop, while picketing and secondary action would only be legal in limited and clearly defined circumstances (Shaw, 1996, p. 187). Changes in personnel have again been important with Tony Blair succeeding the left-wing Michael Meacher as Employment spokesman in the autumn of 1989. Meacher had earlier implied that it would be the policy of a future Labour government to restore the position that had existed before 1979 (Sopel, 1995, p. 108). Perhaps most strikingly of all in view of Kinnock's well publicized personal inclinations, the 1989 party conference abandoned the policy of unilateralism and adopted that of multilateral nuclear disarmament. The party also swung back to support for British membership of the European Community, assisted by the perception that under the President of the Commission, Jacques Delors, that body was now more conducive to Labour's aims and ideals than had once been the case. After Bryan Gould had been replaced as the party's Industry spokesman in October 1989, Labour embraced the idea of membership of the Exchange Rate Mechanism. By the time, therefore, that Britain entered the system in October 1990, this seemed to be a matter of cross-party agreement.

In sum, all this amounted to a dramatic transformation for which Kinnock has perhaps received insufficient recognition. In 1990 the National Institute of Economic and Social Research concluded that 'the economic policy differences between the two major parties are narrower now than they have been for about twenty years' (quoted in Shaw, 1996, p. 185). Overall Labour was unrecognizable as the party which had fought the 1983 General Election under Michael Foot's leadership. It looked electable again. But there was little doubt that the transformation, like that of the Conservative Party after 1945, had been achieved on the terms of the political enemy. A plausible case can be made out for Dennis Kavanagh's conclusion that 'in some respects Mrs Thatcher had more effect on the Labour party than she may have done on the Conservative party' (Kavanagh and Seldon, 1994, p. 11).

The period after the 1987 General Election also showed that the Labour movement itself, and not just its leadership, was returning to the centre ground. By 1990 the parliamentary party, the local constituency parties and even the trade unions were recognizably 'Kinnockite' in their outlook. By the early 1990s the Hard Left had not only lost its control over the NEC, but had all but been eliminated with even the long-serving Tony Benn losing his seat. In 1988 Kinnock crushed Benn's vain attempt to challenge him for the party leadership (and reverse the tide) by a majority of eight to one – and this under the same electoral college which might have swept Benn to victory only a few years earlier. Roy Hattersley held off the challenge of left-winger, Eric Heffer, for the deputy leadership with comparable ease. Not surprisingly, Labour now managed to recover some of the intellectual thrust which had transferred to the SDP and the Alliance in the early to mid 1980s.

Labour approached the General Election of 1992 with some confidence. Opinion polls suggested that it would emerge, at the very least, as the largest single party in the new House of Commons. After thirteen years of Conservative government it seemed reasonable to expect that the electorate would opt for a change, as it had in 1964, especially as the election was fought with the country deep in recession. The 'feel good factor' which psephologists had now identified as the crucial determinant of the outcome of electoral contests was noticeable by its absence. In the circumstances the result was a considerable disappointment from Labour's point of view. Though the party made up substantial ground over its performance in 1987, John Major still emerged with a relatively comfortable overall majority of 21 seats. Strikingly, more people had voted Conservative than had ever supported any party at any previous general election.

One reaction to yet another electoral setback would have been for the Labour Party to swing once more to the left, to emphasize not its similarities with but its differences from the Conservative government. But in the circumstances of 1992 this was never a realistic option. Almost inevitably Neil Kinnock resigned as party leader. It was a sign of the times that, in the contest to succeed him between John Smith and Bryan Gould, the latter – who might at other times have been described as an unrepentant Keynesian – was now seen as the candidate of the Left. His campaign called for a return to a managed economy as the only way to defeat unemployment. He also criticized the restrictions placed upon Britain's capacity to control her own economy as a result of membership of the ERM. But it was also a sign of the times that Smith emerged the comfortable victor. A cautious Scottish lawyer, Smith's leadership was not characterized by any further significant changes of direction, though in general terms the decline of the Left continued, with Smith's close allies, Gordon Brown and Tony Blair, securing election to the NEC. Smith was committed to a patient, long-term strategy to return Labour to government, but he died suddenly in the summer of 1994. His successor, Tony Blair, has done more than any other Labour figure to enshrine the new political consensus of the 1990s.

Blair soon made it clear that he intended to take Labour further towards the centre ground of British politics, even though that 'centre' was now indubitably located, as Keith Joseph had hoped, firmly on the right. One of his first major initiatives as party leader was to propose to the 1994 party conference the replacement of the much venerated Clause IV of the party's constitution, one of Labour's last remaining commitments to traditional socialism. Many believed that this was an irrelevant gesture – after all, few in the Labour movement now talked about public ownership any more; others feared that Blair, like Gaitskell before him, was inviting a rebuff which would damage his leadership. But Blair got his way with surprising ease. A special conference in April 1995 approved his proposed change with just under two-thirds of the total vote. The document which replaced the old Clause IV might, with little exaggeration, have been written by John Major. Labour was now pledged 'to work for a dynamic economy, serving the public interest, in which the enterprise of the market and the rigour of competition are joined with the forces of partnership and cooperation . . . with a thriving public sector and high quality public services' (Shaw, 1996, p. 199).

Meanwhile Labour seemed intent on removing many of its remaining declared differences with the Conservative Party. In its 1992 manifesto Labour had promised to return hospital trusts to NHS control and to end the internal market in the Health Service. Since the election, however, Labour spokesmen have given the impression of accepting even these changes (Kavanagh and Morris, 1994, p. 132). Labour's leading politicians now use that rhetoric of 'standards', 'choice' and 'competition' which was once thought to be the exclusive preserve of the Conservative right. In general, Blair has sought to minimize the number of specific policy proposals made by members of his shadow cabinet in advance of a general election campaign in case these give ammunition to the government to claim that Labour would inevitably have to raise taxes to meet its spending commitments. This strategy owes much to the perception that John Smith's 'shadow budget' at the time of the 1992 election was a vote loser and that Labour must finally shake off the 'tax, spend and borrow' image with which it has so often been associated in the past. In the present context, however, the effect is further to minimize any impression of differences between the Labour and Conservative Parties. Over Europe the rhetoric of political debate implies that fundamental differences separate the two parties. Yet, in truth, divisions are more apparent within those parties than between them, though Labour's readiness to accept the social chapter is a genuine point of differentiation. Both front benches profess their commitment to the European Union, while making it clear that their fundamental concern is to protect British interests. Labour may appear more sympathetic to the goal of monetary union but it has coupled this with conditions about the convergence of the European economies which would, in practice, prove very hard to meet. It is perhaps indicative of the overriding consensus on Europe that many critics of the Maastricht Treaty called for a referendum on this issue (including Lady Thatcher who had previously opposed the idea), precisely because the electorate was not being offered any real choice by the two leading parties.

As in the early 1960s, when Labour and the Conservatives competed with one another in their ability to promote economic growth through planning, Labour now seeks to rival the Tories' ability to implement a free-market system, a task eased by the Conservative government's loss of economic credibility after the ERM débâcle of September 1992. 'We are the party that understands and can run a dynamic market economy', Blair proclaimed in a newspaper interview in October 1994. Despite the use of jargon phrases such as 'the stakeholder society', which recalled for many the rhetoric of Harold Wilson, there is little evidence that Labour under Tony Blair poses an ideological divide from the Conservatives or offers the vision of a genuinely different sort of society from that which developed during the 1980s. So clear had the convergence between the two parties become by 1995 that right-wing Tories began to proclaim the need to place 'clear blue water' between themselves and Labour, and it was in this spirit that John Redwood challenged John Major for the Conservative leadership that summer. Under the headline 'Why all good Tories should vote Labour', the journalist Robert Harris declared that the next general election offers Conservatives a unique opportunity 'to make Margaret Thatcher's dream of a Britain free from socialism a reality' (R. Harris, 1996). Blair has even expressed a qualified admiration for Margaret Thatcher – something which it is difficult to imagine passing the lips of any previous Labour leader. With the declared aim of modernizing the party – which he now proudly describes as 'New Labour' – Blair has sought to weaken the traditional links between Labour and the trade union movement and promises to continue this process of liberation. The TUC, we are told, should expect no special relationship with a future Blair government. Voices from the left have indicated their disquiet with the drift of Labour politics, as have old-fashioned Keynesians such as Roy Hattersley, but, at the time of writing, Blair seems to have established an ascendancy over his party unrivalled by any party leader of recent times. Dennis Kavanagh's words, written in 1994, seem even more apposite two years on. 'In many respects the party system since 1990 has failed to articulate well defined choices between the major parties on economic management, on the European Community and on most of the public services'(Kavanagh and Seldon, 1994, p. 153).

Conclusion

The central argument of this book has been that a political consensus emerged as a product of the experience of the Second World War (though its shape was by no means complete in 1945), and that it dominated the 1950s and 1960s, surviving into the 1970s under increasing strain. It has been shown that 'adversarial politics' and 'consensus politics' were by no means mutually exclusive terms (Wilton, 1990, p. 27). During this period 'what stands out is not the rhetoric of political controversy but the continuity in policy choice' (Kavanagh and Morris, 1994, p. 130). 'As during the war, *uncompromising* dissent was largely confined to groups of party members remote from power' (Searle, 1995, p. 225). But the term 'consensus' had ceased to be a useful framework of historical analysis by the time of the General Election of 1979. This post-war consensus collapsed in the face of the emergence of new problems to which it appeared not to have the answers, and in the light of increasing evidence that it could not even tackle those problems which it had once seemed purpose-built to resolve.

It has then been argued that, after a period of marked polarization during the 1980s, when it was the right of the Conservative Party and the left of Labour which were in the ascendant, there has gradually emerged a new consensus which is shaping the politics of the 1990s. It is at least arguable that the new consensus is even closer than the first. In relation to the post-war consensus it could certainly be suggested that Labour's leaders, notwithstanding their short-term pragmatism, retained a long-term vision of the transformation of British society which differentiated them from the Tories. It seems unlikely that this distinction applies to the Labour leadership of the mid-1990s. According to Nigel Lawson, Tony Blair is 'quite definitely the least socialist leader the Labour Party has ever had' (quoted in Rentoul, 1995, p. 163). Like that which had developed by 1951, this second consensus involves a movement by both parties towards a common ground. 'If the parties are close together', claims Ian Gilmour, 'they will necessarily be moderate. To be close together, they both have to be centrist, and centrism entails moderation' (Gilmour, 1983, p. 197). This rather misses the point. The perception of moderation is not static. The 'centre ground' of 1951 would have been regarded as extreme before the war. The 'centre ground' of 1996 would have been similarly seen in the 1960s. The earlier consensus was firmly fixed in a centre–left position; its successor is of the centre–right. In both cases an important factor in its creation was the adaptation of one party to electoral defeat. Labour's four successive losses – in 1979 and more particularly in 1983, 1987, and 1992 – have had a sobering effect, just as did the Conservative débâcle of 1945. Any party which aspires to government must take account of the lessons of defeat and reflect upon the verdict of the voters. This is not surprising. As Quintin Hogg once wrote: 'There is no copyright in truth and what is controversial politics at one moment may after experience and reflection easily become common ground' (Hailsham, 1959, p. 16).

The story is incomplete and in some ways unproven to the extent that the Labour Party was never in a position in the 1980s to be able to implement its left-wing alternative to the consensus politics of earlier years. Indeed, it is possible that had a Labour government been elected in 1983 or 1987 it would have been obliged, like its predecessor of 1974, to trim its socialist sails in the face of the realities of the prevailing situation. It has, after all, been one of the purposes of this book to stress the differences which often occur between what a party says in opposition and what in practice it does in power. As one Whitehall insider has put it, 'when a government is in opposition, it has a different view of . . . the real world from the next day after it's got into office. And therefore the strategies one works out in opposition . . . almost inevitably need modification when they are faced with the real facts of life' (Bruce-Gardyne, 1974, p. 105). The result might well have been a centrist government of the 1980s in the Wilson–Callaghan mould, which could even have been forced by the climate of world opinion to embrace some of the ideas of the New Right. Similarly, as Anthony Seldon has written, 'until Labour forms a government, and having done so decides to continue with the Conservatives' policies, talk of a new consensus is premature. It is continuity of government policies between both parties *in office* which defines consensus' (Seldon, 1994, p. 57). It remains theoretically possible (as some Conservatives like to claim – 'New Labour, new danger') that a Blair government would revert to its natural socialist instincts and make all talk of a new post-Thatcherite consensus redundant. But such a development would involve one of the most astonishing political transformations of modern times.

All but the implacable 'Hard Left' now seem convinced that Labour would never win another election with some of the policies presented to the electorate in 1983 and 1987. Eleven years of government under Mrs Thatcher, in most respects consolidated by six years under her successor, have had a remarkable effect in shifting the political goal-posts firmly, and possibly irreversibly, to the right, particularly since many governments across the world have behaved in a very similar fashion. During the later 1980s even left-of-centre governments in France, Spain and Australasia all found themselves adopting recognizably New Right policies (Kavanagh and Seldon, 1994, p. 12). In the 1990s the former command economies of eastern Europe have adopted the practices and ethos of the market with gusto. Back in the 1970s Sir Keith Joseph spoke of the need to establish a new 'common ground' to the right of centre. There is clear evidence that this has now become a reality. A new set of parameters has come into existence within which a future Labour government would have to operate. Most commentators agreed that Labour fought an effective campaign in the General Election of 1987. Its reward – barely 30 per cent of the popular vote – showed that it was Labour's policies which were the problem. The subsequent policy review resulted in a Labour Party which was almost unrecognizable from the one which Michael Foot took into battle in 1983. Yet Labour's further defeat in 1992 was taken to mean that the party still had some way to go in the process of adapting to the new political climate. Further important policy changes resulted.

For nearly a decade now, it has been difficult to see a future Labour government being able, even if it so wished, completely to reverse the changes effected by the Conservatives since 1979. Further nationalization has ceased to be practical politics. Labour could not reintroduce exchange controls in a world which has largely abandoned them. Any hopes of socialism in one country thus seem no more than the pipe-dream of a few extremists of the Far Left. The reduction in trade union power has proved so popular – even among trade unionists – that a Labour government would seek to turn back the clock at its peril. The once reviled policy of selling council houses is now an established fact. No Labour government would dare to pursue policies which ran the risk of inflation on the scale of the 1970s. Indeed, if Labour really is more enthusiastic than the Conservatives about a single European currency, it may find itself in government having to pursue even stricter monetary control than the present Conservative government in order to meet the criteria laid down in the Maastricht Treaty. Such a commitment would certainly preclude any increases in overall public expenditure. In general terms the increasing internationalization of the world economy is bound to reduce the scope for manoeuvre of any future government of no matter which party political complexion. Similarly, economic realities will circumscribe the range of policy options for Labour and Conservative alike. It is no longer only the Right which 'wonders whether the stubborn problems of poverty and deprivation require a new look at universal schemes of welfare provision'. Already the vocabulary of 'selectivity' and 'targeting' – once the preserve of the Conservative free-marketeer – has been heard emanating from Labour's Commission on Social Justice (Kavanagh and Morris, 1994, p. 133).

Some changes of attitude occurred fairly early on in the Thatcher era. When in 1981 the SDP called for a reinstatement of Keynesianism, Ralf Dahrendorf joked that the party seemed to be 'promising a better past'. That same year the TUC put forward a five-year programme for *The Reconstruction of Industry*. It was a reflection of its declining faith in Keynesian policies of public investment that the TUC's plan would have generated no more than half a million jobs in five years (Peden, 1985, p. 232). Over a period of time the political debate in Britain moved on to the ground of who could best run a market economy. It was 'no longer about whether we have a market economy or a socialist one' (Ridley, 1991, p. 255). Interviewed in April 1992, John Major put it in these terms: 'Socialism of course is dead and gone. Finished, passed, out of the window. Nobody believes in it any more. Nobody. Not in this country, not abroad. It is now a museum piece, nothing more. Time has passed it by.' Even allowing for the rhetoric of the political partisan there is something in this assessment.

One consequence of Labour's coming to terms with the new realities has been a loss of support for the Social and Liberal Democrats since the 1987 election. The Liberal Democrats secured six million votes in 1992 as against 7.3 million for the Alliance in 1987, 18.3 per cent of the popular vote compared with 22.5 per cent. More importantly, questions have been asked as to whether Labour's movement to the right has left any room in the centre ground for the Liberal Democrats, a question partially answered by the spectacle of Lord Jenkins, the Liberal Democrat leader in the upper chamber, acting as an unofficial adviser and mentor to Tony Blair. When Labour and the Conservatives contest 'the middle ground', wherever that middle ground is placed on the political spectrum at any given moment, the centre parties have always been the most obvious casualties.

So future historians will almost certainly write of the rise and fall and rebirth of consensus politics, with 1979 as the pivotal year, just as 1945 was for an earlier era. They will, however, regard these years as indicators rather than as fundamental dividing lines. This book has attempted to show that, however important the Attlee and Thatcher governments were in introducing far-reaching changes which set the agenda for the administrations which followed them, political culture tends to evolve over a period of time and is not necessarily or in all respects dependent on changes of government. The new consensus will not imply, any more than did its predecessor, a total uniformity of outlook, policy and ambition between the two major parties. Using such unrealistic criteria, some have already questioned its existence (Riddell, 1993). But Churchill's words to the American Congress in 1952 probably still hold true. While Labour's 'social democracy' and the Tories' 'free enterprise' give plenty of room for argument, they 'fortunately overlap quite a lot in practice' (quoted in Ramsden, 1987, p. 52).

One final question clearly confronts the student of British politics since 1945. The debate over the very existence of a post-war consensus is clearly one of considerable historical importance. In recent years, however, it has also taken on a contemporary political significance. Just as there is not full agreement on whether the consensus actually existed, there is no agreement among those who believe that it did exist on the effect which it had on Britain's post-war development. In short, was the consensus of the period 1945–70 a good thing or not? The evidence is contradictory. On the one hand, there can be no doubt that these years witnessed very substantial progress, not least in the material welfare of the British people. The creation of the welfare state, so soon after the enormous sacrifices entailed in the Second World War, was itself no small achievement. Average real earnings rose by 20 per cent between 1951 and 1959, so that by the end of the decade Prime Minister Macmillan could, with some considerable justification, proclaim that 'most of our people have never had it so good'. Nor was this advance at the expense of the less fortunate in society. Between 1945 and 1970 unemployment, the great scourge of the inter-war era, averaged less than 3 per cent. Yet, in comparison with many of her competitors, this was also, as has been seen, a period in which Britain's long-term relative decline accelerated. Between 1953 and 1960 the country's share of world manufactured exports fell from 20 to 15 per cent. Over the same period West Germany's share rose from 15 to 19 per cent. French exports increased three times as fast and West Germany's and Italy's six times as fast as did Britain's in these years. In 1945 Britain was rightly regarded as one of the world's great powers. By 1970 no serious observer could still maintain such a belief.

The argument goes yet further. It is possible to suggest that it was the policies of the consensus years which actually contributed to Britain's decline – that the policy-makers of the 1950s and 1960s failed to grapple with the country's underlying problems, particularly in the economy, with the result that when the moment of reckoning arrived in the 1970s and 1980s it proved all the more acute and painful. The overmanned and under-funded state of the British industrial base which awaited its inevitable fate in the crises of these years stands at the most poignant illustration. In short, the consensus may not simply have coincided with a period of relative decline; it may have helped cause it. Correlli Barnett has been the most eloquent advocate of this point of view. His argument is that by opting for the temptations of a 'New Jerusalem' after 1945 – a 'better, more equal Britain to be built when there were blue birds over the white cliffs of Dover' – the country's rulers wasted a unique opportunity to tackle the root causes of her long-term industrial decline. When Britain needed to invest in her industry and workforce, and do something about the anti-industrial ethos of her education system, she chose instead to create the welfare state. But that in turn ultimately produced a dependency culture – a 'subliterate, unskilled, unhealthy and institutionalized proletariat hanging on the nipple of state materialism' (C. Barnett, 1986, pp. 276, 304). All the key elements of the post-war consensus – the welfare state, the managed economy, the maintenance of the semblance of great power status – were, in Barnett's view, wrong choices. They constituted a 'total strategy of British dreams, British illusions and British overstretch' (C. Barnett, 1995, p. 398). Though forcefully argued, this thesis has not gone unchallenged, not least because other European nations managed to combine policies of industrial regeneration with increased spending on welfare provision (J. Harris, 1991).

It is largely the political standpoint of the contemporary observer which determines the interpretation he gives to the years of consensus. For the New Right of the 1970s and 1980s the consensus marked the period in which the Conservative Party meekly acquiesced in the drift towards an ever more collectivist and socialistic state, while participating in a conspiracy of rising inflation. For the Bennite or 'hard' left of the Labour Party the consensus involved the abandonment of genuinely socialist goals and a too ready acceptance of a fundamentally capitalist society. By contrast, and while Labour and Conservatives increasingly abandoned the centre ground in the course of the 1970s, others came to regard the post-war years with an affectionate nostalgia. Implicit in the late Lord Stockton's criticisms of Mrs Thatcher's government was the presumption that the country's performance had deteriorated since the time he was prime minister. Thus both supporters and detractors of the Thatcher and Major governments have had good reason to exaggerate the extent to which 1979 marks a break with the past. Their analyses tend to make the ending of the consensus more clear-cut and complete than was perhaps the case.

The most objective assessment perhaps tackles the question in a rather different way. It was in all probability inevitable that something like the post-war consensus would emerge. The generation which had grown up in the depression years of the 1930s, fought the war and experienced the continuing privations which this entailed, demanded that politicians should focus their attention just as soon as it was possible on the creation of a better world. Those who, with the inestimable benefits of hindsight, look back on the supposed missed opportunities of the 1950s and 1960s fail to take note of what was politically possible within a democracy, particularly one which was anxious to enjoy the supposed fruits of the military victory achieved at such great cost. 'There is no alternative' was a political phrase closely associated with the policies and convictions of Margaret Thatcher. Perhaps, however, it was equally appropriate to the years of consensus after 1945. In due course, no doubt, a lively debate will also develop around the merits or otherwise of the new consensus of the 1990s. Political partisans will already hold strong views. At the time of writing, however, it is still too early for the cautious historian to offer even a tentative judgement.

Chronology

1939	September	Outbreak of war between Britain and Germany.
1940	May	Fall of Neville Chamberlain's National Government and formation of all-party coalition under Winston Churchill.
	May–June	Evacuation of British army from Dunkirk.
	July–September	Battle of Britain.
1941	June	Germany attacks the Soviet Union.
	December	United States enters the war after Japanese attack on Pearl Harbor.
1942	February	Singapore surrenders to the Japanese.
	October–November	Battle of El Alamein.
	November	Allied invasion of North Africa.
	December	Publication of the Beveridge Report.
1943	February	Parliament debates Beveridge Report
	March	Churchill broadcast commits government to schemes of social improvement. Tory Reform Committee formally constituted.
	July	White Paper on education.

1944	February	White Paper on a national health service.
	May	White Paper on employment.
	June	D-Day. Allies invade Normandy.
	August	Butler's Education bill becomes law.
	October	Labour's NEC commits Labour to fight next election as independent party.
1945	February	Yalta Conference between Churchill, Roosevelt and Stalin.
	April	Hitler commits suicide.
	May	VE Day. Germany capitulates.
		Churchill disbands coalition and forms caretaker government pending a general election.
	July	General election.
		Potsdam Conference between Churchill, Truman and Stalin.
		Formation of Attlee's Labour government.
	August	Atomic bombs dropped on Hiroshima and Nagasaki.
		Japan surrenders. End of Second World War.
	October–November	Dock Strike.
	December	Britain signs agreement with USA for loan for post-war reconstruction.
1946	March	Bank of England nationalized.
		Churchill delivers Iron Curtain speech.
	July	Coal Nationalization Bill enacted.
	August	National Insurance Bill enacted.
	November	King's Speech announces nationalization of railways, ports, long-distance road transport and inland waterways.
1947	January	National Coal Board comes into being.
		Cable and Wireless nationalized.
		Cabinet committee authorizes manufacture of British atomic bomb.
	March	Moscow conference of foreign ministers.
	May	Conservative Party publishes *Industrial Charter*.

	June	General Marshall's Harvard speech on aid to Europe.
	August	British rule ends in India.
	September	Britain announces relinquishment of Palestine mandate.
	November	Cripps becomes Chancellor of the Exchequer.
1948	January	Railways nationalized.
	April	Electricity nationalized.
	July	National Health Service inaugurated. Berlin blockade begins.
	November	Harold Wilson announces 'bonfire of controls'.
1949	April	NATO treaty signed in Washington.
	May	Gas nationalization comes into effect.
	September	Pound devalued from $4.03 to $2.80.
	November	Iron and steel bill enacted though nationalization is delayed until 1951.
1950	February	General election. Labour majority greatly reduced.
	June	Cabinet rejects Schuman Plan for European Coal and Steel Community. Korean War begins.
	October	Cripps resigns and is succeeded by Gaitskell.
1951	February	Iron and steel nationalization takes effect.
	April	Bevan, Wilson and Freeman resign over health service charges and scale of defence spending.
	October	General election produces overall Conservative majority of 17.
1952	February	Plan Robot to make sterling convertible defeated.
	May	Iain Macleod becomes Minister of Health.
	October	British atomic bomb detonated at Monte Bello, Australia.

1953	May	British Road Services and iron and steel industries denationalized.
	December	Macmillan achieves target of 300,000 new houses a year.
1954	February	Article in the *Economist* coins the phrase 'Butskellism'.
	October	Rationing formally ended.
1955	April	Churchill retires and is succeeded by Eden.
	May	General election. Conservatives secure overall majority of 58.
	July	First post-war hospital building programme initiated.
	October	Butler forced to increase taxes in supplementary budget.
	December	Attlee resigns as Labour leader and is succeeded by Gaitskell.
1956	January	Guillebaud Committee report on NHS.
	March	White Paper *The Economic Implications of Full Employment*, published.
	July	Suez Canal Company nationalized.
	October–November	Suez Crisis.
	December	Anglo-French forces leave Suez.
1957	January	Eden resigns as prime minister and is succeeded by Macmillan.
	March	Treaty of Rome signed setting up European Economic Community.
	April	Defence White Paper places greater emphasis on nuclear deterrent.
	May	British hydrogen bomb exploded at Christmas Island.
	June	Rent Act becomes law.
	July	Macmillan delivers 'never had it so good' speech in Bedford.

1958	January	Thorneycroft, Powell and Birch resign as Treasury ministers.
	October	Rent Act comes into operation.
1959	April	Amory's budget takes 9d off income tax.
	July	TGWU endorses unilateral nuclear disarmament.
	October	General election; Conservatives re-elected with overall majority of 100.
		Gaitskell urges Labour Party Conference to abandon Clause IV of the Labour constitution.
1960	February	Macmillan makes 'Winds of Change' speech in Cape Town.
	April	Neutral budget; deflation rejected.
	July	Labour's NEC decides to keep Clause IV.
		Selwyn Lloyd succeeds Heathcoat Amory as Chancellor.
	October	Labour Party Conference endorses unilateral nuclear disarmament.
1961	July	Lloyd announces 'pay pause'; government spending checked.
	August	Britain applies to join European Economic Community.
	October	Gaitskell secures reversal of unilateralist policy at Labour Party Conference.
	November	Government introduces bill to restrict Commonwealth immigration.
1962	February	National Economic Development Council set up.
	March	Stunning Liberal victory in Orpington by-election.
		Formal 'pay pause' replaced by 'guiding light' for wage increases.

	July	'Night of the long knives'; Macmillan sacks seven cabinet ministers; Maudling becomes Chancellor.
		National Incomes Commission set up.
1963	January	De Gaulle vetoes Britain's first application to join EEC.
		Hugh Gaitskell dies and is succeeded by Harold Wilson as Labour leader in February.
	February	NEDC approves 4 per cent target growth rate.
	June	Profumo forced to resign as War Minister.
	October	Macmillan resigns as Conservative Party Conference opens. Lord Home 'emerges' as his successor.
1964	July	Resale Price Maintenance Act comes into force.
	October	General election sees return of Labour government with overall majority of five.
	November	Sterling crisis; budget increases pensions and abolishes prescription charges.
1965	February	Donovan Commission on trade unions set up.
		Prices and Incomes Board established.
	July	Government circular on comprehensive schools.
		Douglas-Home resigns as Conservative leader and is succeeded by Edward Heath.
	August	White Paper on immigration controls.
	September	National Plan published.
	November	Death penalty abolished.
1966	January	White Paper on Industrial Reorganization Corporation.
	March	General election; Labour increases overall majority to 97.
	May	State of Emergency over seamen's dispute.

	July	Sterling crisis; prices and incomes legislation introduced.
1967	March	Iron and steel industries renationalized.
	May	Britain makes second application to join EEC.
	October	Abortion Act.
	November	Sterling crisis; pound devalued from $2.80 to $2.40.
		De Gaulle blocks Britain's EEC application.
1968	January	Raising of school-leaving age postponed.
	March	Commonwealth Immigration Act.
	April	Enoch Powell dismissed from shadow cabinet.
	June	Donovan Report published.
	July	Defence White Paper greatly reduces Britain's role outside Europe.
	October	Road transport renationalized.
1969	January	White Paper, *In Place of Strife*, published.
	June	*In Place of Strife* abandoned.
	August	British troops sent into Northern Ireland.
1970	January	Conservative shadow cabinet meets at Selsdon Park.
	June	General election gives Conservatives comfortable overall majority.
		EEC negotiations recommence.
	July	Chancellor Iain Macleod dies; succeeded by Anthony Barber.
	December	Industrial Relations Bill published.
1971	February	Rolls Royce nationalized following bankruptcy.
	August	Industrial Relations Act becomes law.
		Sterling floated within fixed range.
1972	January	Unemployment exceeds one million.
		Strike by National Union of Mineworkers.

February	Wilberforce Report settles strike to miners' satisfaction.
April	Roy Jenkins resigns as Labour's deputy leader.
June	Pound floated freely.
November	Heath announces 90 day pay and prices freeze.

1973

January	Britain joins EEC.
February	Labour Party and TUC launch 'Social Contract'.
April	Stage II of prices and incomes policy.
November	Miners start overtime ban.
December	Three-day week introduced.

1974

February	NUM call all-out strike. General election leaves Labour largest single party but without overall majority.
March	Heath resigns after efforts to form Conservative-Liberal coalition; Labour takes office under Wilson. Miners' strike settled.
April	EEC renegotiation begins.
October	General election gives Labour overall majority of 3.
December	Retail prices up 19 per cent and wages 29 per cent over last twelve months.

1975

February	Margaret Thatcher defeats Heath for Conservative leadership.
April	Special Labour Party Conference calls for 'no' vote in EEC referendum.
June	67 per cent 'yes' vote in EEC referendum. Varley replaces Benn as Industry Secretary.
July	Voluntary pay policy announced. Unemployment passes one million mark.
August	Price rises running at 26.9 per cent per annum.

	November	Cash limits to be applied to public expenditure.
1976	February	Public expenditure cuts of £1000m. for 1977-8.
	March	Wilson resigns.
	April	James Callaghan becomes prime minister.
	May	TUC accepts further twelve months of wage restraint.
	July	Further public spending cuts.
	September	Jenkins resigns as Home Secretary to take up EEC presidency.
		Callaghan appears to renounce Keynesianism in Labour Party Conference speech.
	December	Cabinet accepts IMF terms for loan.
1977	March	Aircraft and shipbuilding industries nationalized.
		Lib-Lab Pact formed.
	July	Chancellor Healey announces Phase III of Incomes Policy.
	October	Reg Prentice leaves Labour Party.
1978	February	Inflation rate falls below 10 per cent.
	July	White Paper sets out 5 per cent limit for Stage IV of Incomes Policy.
	October	Labour Party Conference rejects 5 per cent wage limit.
1979	January–February	Winter of discontent; widespread public sector strikes.
	March	Government defeated 311-310 on vote of no confidence.
	May	General election; Conservatives under Mrs Thatcher returned with overall majority of 43.
	June	Howe's first budget cuts income tax and public expenditure, but raises VAT.
	November	Roy Jenkins calls in Dimbleby Lecture for realignment of the 'radical centre'.

1980	April	Inflation running at 21.8 per cent per annum.
	May	British Aerospace privatized.
	August	Housing bill enacted, giving tenants the right to buy council houses.
	October	Unemployment tops 2 million. Callaghan resigns as Labour leader.
	November	Michael Foot elected Labour leader.
1981	January	Labour Party Special Conference adopts electoral college for election of future leaders and their deputies.
	March	Budget cuts £3,500m. from PSBR. Social Democratic Party launched.
	June	SDP-Liberal Alliance formed.
	July	Riots in Liverpool and Manchester.
1982	January	Employment Bill gives compensation to workers sacked for refusing to join a closed shop.
	April	Argentine invasion of Falkland Islands.
	June	British troops recapture Falkland Islands.
	July	Roy Jenkins elected SDP leader.
1983	January	Inflation down to 5.4 per cent.
	June	General election; Conservative majority increases to 144; Nigel Lawson succeeds Howe as Chancellor of the Exchequer. Inflation down to 3.7 per cent. David Owen elected leader of SDP.
	October	Neil Kinnock replaces Foot as Labour leader.
1984	March	Miners' strike begins.
	April	Telecommunications bill to privatize British Telecom.
	October	IRA bomb at Grand Hotel, Brighton, during Conservative Party Conference.
	November	Shares in British Telecom oversubscribed.

	December	Keith Joseph forced to abandon plans for higher parental contributions to student maintenance.
1985	March	Miners' strike ends.
	May	Francis Pym launches 'Centre Forward' in 'One Nation' tradition.
	June	Green Paper on Social Security reform.
	October	Privatization of National Bus Company.
	November	Anglo-Irish Agreement.
1986	January	Michael Heseltine resigns from cabinet.
	February	Mrs Thatcher signs Single European Act.
		Unemployment at over 3.4 million.
	March	Lawson reduces standard rate income tax to 29 per cent.
	October	Trustee Savings Bank sold to public.
	December	British Gas privatized.
1987	January	British Airways privatized.
	March	Income tax reduced to 27 per cent.
	April	Unemployment falls for eighth consecutive month.
	June	General election; overall Conservative majority of 101.
		Unemployment falls below 3 million.
		David Steel calls for fusion between SDP and Liberals.
1988	March	Standard rate of income tax cut to 25 per cent; top rate to 40 per cent.
	July	Alan Walters returns as Mrs Thatcher's economic adviser.
	September	Mrs Thatcher makes Bruges speech opposing European federalism.
1989	January	White Paper on NHS.
	May	Labour publishes review document, *Meet the Challenge, Make the Change.*

	July	Geoffrey Howe 'demoted' from Foreign Office to post of Deputy Prime Minister.
	October	Lawson resigns as Chancellor; succeeded by John Major.
	November	Demolition of Berlin Wall begins, signalling end of Cold War.
1990	April	Community Charge introduced.
	June	SDP disbanded.
	October	Britain joins Exchange Rate Mechanism.
	November	Geoffrey Howe resigns from government. Michael Heseltine challenges Mrs Thatcher for Conservative leadership. Mrs Thatcher resigns. John Major defeats Heseltine and Douglas Hurd to become leader and prime minister.
1991	January–February	Gulf War.
	April	Far-reaching reforms of the NHS announced.
	December	Maastricht Treaty negotiations.
1992	April	General election; Conservatives under John Major returned with reduced overall majority of 21.
	July	John Smith elected to succeed Neil Kinnock as Labour leader.
	September	Britain forced to withdraw from Exchange Rate Mechanism.
1993	July	Government defeated in Commons on Social Chapter but wins subsequent confidence vote.
	August	Britain ratifies Maastricht Treaty.
	November	Major calls for 'back to basics' at Conservative Party Conference.
	December	Downing Street Declaration launches new Northern Ireland peace initiative.

1994	May	John Smith dies suddenly.
	June	Significant Conservative losses in European elections.
	July	Tony Blair elected Labour leader.
	August	IRA ceasefire.
	October	Blair calls for Labour to modernize its constitution.
	November	Plans to privatize Post Office abandoned.
1995	March	Remaining 40 per cent holding in electricity generating companies sold off.
	April	Special Labour Party Conference replaces Clause IV of constitution.
	May	Conservatives sustain worst defeat in post-war history in local council elections for England and Wales.
		White Paper proposes privatization of nuclear power.
	June	Major resigns Conservative leadership, but puts his name forward for re-election.
	July	Major defeats John Redwood to retain Conservative leadership.
	August	Widespread criticism within Labour Party of Blair's style of leadership.
	September	Kevin McNamara resigns from Labour front bench in opposition to bi-partisan policy on Northern Ireland.
1996	February	First privatized passenger trains for fifty years.
	March	European crisis over British beef.
	May	Conservatives sustain further losses in local elections.
	July	Nuclear power generation privatized.
	December	Conservatives lose their Commons majority; continuing turmoil within the party over Europe.

Bibliography and References

The literature on post-war British political history is already enormous and growing all the time. The list of works detailed below is restricted to books and articles referred to in the text. Those who wish to keep up with an ever expanding historiography are urged to consult two important journals, *Twentieth Century British History* and *Contemporary British History* (formerly *Contemporary Record*)

Addison, Paul 1975: *The Road to 1945: British Politics and the Second World War*. London: Cape.

Addison, Paul 1985: *Now the War is Over*. London: Cape.

Addison, Paul 1992: *Churchill on the Home Front*. London: Cape.

Addison, Paul 1993: Consensus Revisited. *Twentieth Century British History*, 4, pp. 91–4.

Anderson, Bruce 1991: *John Major: The Making of the Prime Minister*. London: Fourth Estate.

Artis, M., Cobham, D. and Wickham-Jones, M. 1992: Social Democracy in Hard Times: The Economic Record of the Labour Government 1974–1979. *Twentieth Century British History*, 3, pp. 32–58.

Attlee, Clement 1954: *As it Happened*. London: Heinemann.

Ball, Stuart 1995: *The Conservative Party and British Politics, 1902–1951*. London: Longman.

Barnett, Correlli 1986: *The Audit of War*. London: Macmillan.

Barnett, Correlli 1995: *The Lost Victory*. London: Macmillan.

Barnett, Joel 1982: *Inside the Treasury*. London: Deutsch.

Beer, Samuel 1965: *Modern British Politics*. London: Faber.

Bell, Daniel 1960: *The End of Ideology*. Illinois: Free Press.

Benn, Tony 1988: *Office Without Power. Diaries 1968–72*. London: Hutchinson.

Benn, Tony 1989: *Against the Tide. Diaries 1973–6*. London: Hutchinson.

Biffen, John 1988: The Post-war Consensus. *Contemporary Record*, 2, 1, p. 16.

Bradley, Ian 1981: *Breaking the Mould*. Oxford: Martin Robertson.

Brittan, Samuel 1964: *The Treasury under the Tories, 1951–1964*. Harmondsworth: Penguin.

Brittan, Samuel 1971: *Steering the Economy*. New York: The Library Press.

Brooke, Stephen 1992: *Labour's War: The Labour Party during the Second World War*. Oxford: Clarendon Press.

Brooke, Stephen 1995: The Labour Party and the 1945 General Election. *Contemporary Record*, 9, pp. 1–21.

Bruce-Gardyne, Jock 1974: *Whatever Happened to the Quiet Revolution*. London: Charles Knight.

Bruce-Gardyne, Jock 1984: *Mrs Thatcher's First Administration*. London: Macmillan.

Bullock, Alan 1983: *Ernest Bevin: Foreign Secretary 1945–1951*. London: Heinemann.

Burgess, Simon and Alderman, Geoffrey 1990: Centre for Policy Studies. *Contemporary Record*, 4, 2, pp. 14–15.

Burk, Kathleen and Cairncross, Alec 1992: *'Goodbye, Great Britain': the 1976 IMF Crisis*. New Haven: Yale University Press.

Burridge, Trevor 1985: *Clement Attlee*. London: Cape.

Butler, David 1955: *The British General Election of 1955*. London: Cass.

Butler, David 1989: *British General Elections since 1945*. Oxford: Basil Blackwell.

Butler, R. A. [Lord] 1971: *The Art of the Possible*. London: Hamilton.

Byrnes, James 1947: *Speaking Frankly*. London: Heinemann.

Cairncross, Alec 1985: *Years of Recovery*. London: Methuen.

Callaghan, James 1987: *Time and Chance*. London: Collins.

Campbell, John 1987: *Nye Bevan and the Mirage of British Socialism*. London: Weidenfeld & Nicolson.

Campbell, John 1993: *Edward Heath*. London: Cape.

Castle, Barbara 1980: *The Castle Diaries 1974–76*. London: Weidenfeld & Nicolson.

Castle, Barbara 1984: *The Castle Diaries 1964–70*. London: Weidenfeld & Nicolson.

Castle, Barbara 1993: *Fighting All the Way*. London: Macmillan.

Chester, Norman 1975: *The Nationalisation of British Industry 1945–51*. London: HMSO.

Childs, David 1986: *Britain Since 1945: A Political History*. London: Benn.

Coates, David 1980: *Labour in Power? A Study of the Labour Government 1974–1979*. London: Longman.

Colville, John 1981: *The Churchillians*. London: Weidenfeld and Nicolson.

Coopey, Richard, Fielding, Steven and Tiratsoo, Nick (eds) 1993: *The Wilson Government 1964–1970*. London: Pinter.

Cosgrave, Patrick 1989: *The Lives of Enoch Powell*. London: Bodley Head.

Cosgrave, Patrick 1992: *The Strange Death of Socialist Britain*. London: Constable.

Crewe, Ivor 1990: The Policy Agenda. *Contemporary Record*, 3, 3, pp. 2–7.

Crossman, Richard 1981: *The Backbench Diaries of Richard Crossman*. ed. Janet Morgan. London: Hamilton.

Daly, Gerard 1993: The Campaign for Labour Victory and the Origins of the SDP. *Contemporary Record*, 7, pp. 282–305.

Davis Smith, Justin 1990: *The Attlee and Churchill Administrations and Industrial Unrest*. London: Pinter.

Donoughue, Bernard 1987: *Prime Minister: The Conduct of Policy under Harold Wilson and James Callaghan*. London: Cape.

Dorey, Peter 1991: Thatcherism's Impact on Trade Unions. *Contemporary Record*, 4, 4, pp. 9–11.

Dorey, Peter 1995: *British Politics since 1945*. Oxford: Blackwell Publishers.

Duff, Peggy 1971: *Left, Left, Left: A Personal Account of Six Protest Campaigns, 1945–65*. London: Allison & Busby.

Dutton, David 1985: *Austen Chamberlain: Gentleman in Politics*. Bolton: Ross Anderson.

Dutton, David 1996: *Anthony Eden: A Life and Reputation*. London: Arnold.

Eatwell, Roger 1979: *The 1945–1951 Labour Governments*. London: Batsford.

Eden, Sir Anthony 1960: *Full Circle*. London: Cassell.

Fielding, Steven 1992: What did 'the People' want?: The Meaning of the 1945 General Election. *Historical Journal*, 35, pp. 623–39.

Fielding, Steven, Thompson, Peter and Tiratsoo, Nick 1995: *England Arise*. Manchester: Manchester University Press.

Fisher, Nigel 1973: *Iain Macleod*. London: Deutsch.
Gilbert, Martin 1988: *Winston S. Churchill: Never Despair* London: Heinemann.
Gilmour, Ian 1983: *Britain Can Work*. Oxford: Martin Robertson.
Gorst, Anthony, Johnman, Lewis and Lucas, W. Scott (eds) 1991: *Contemporary British History 1931–1961*. London: Pinter.
Gough, I. 1979: *The Political Economy of the Welfare State*. London: Macmillan.
Gowing, Margaret 1974: *Independence and Deterrence: Britain and Atomic Energy 1945–1952*, vol. I. London: Macmillan.
Greenwood, Sean 1992: *Britain and European Cooperation since 1945*. Oxford: Basil Blackwell.
Hailsham, Lord 1959: *The Conservative Case*. Harmondsworth: Penguin.
Halcrow, Morrison 1989: *Keith Joseph: A Single Mind.* London: Macmillan.
Harris, José 1983: Did British Workers want the Welfare State, in Winter, Jay (ed.): *The Working Class in Modern British History*. Cambridge: Cambridge University Press.
Harris, José 1991: Enterprise and the Welfare State, in Gourvish, Terry and O'Day, Alan (eds): *Britain since 1945*. London: Macmillan.
Harris, Kenneth 1982: *Attlee*. London: Weidenfeld & Nicolson.
Harris, Robert 1996: Why all good Tories should vote Labour. *Sunday Times* 5 May 1996.
Harvey, John (ed.) 1978: *The War Diaries of Oliver Harvey*. London: Collins.
Haseler, Stephen 1980: *The Tragedy of Labour*. Oxford: Blackwell.
Healey, Denis 1990: *The Time of My Life*. Harmondsworth: Penguin.
Hennessy, Peter 1992: *Never Again: Britain 1945–51*. London: Cape.
Hennessy, Peter and Seldon, Anthony (eds) 1987: *Ruling Performance: British Governments from Attlee to Thatcher*. Oxford: Basil Blackwell.
Holmes, Martin 1985a: *The Labour Government, 1974–79: Political Aims and Economic Reality*. London: Macmillan.
Holmes, Martin 1985b: *The First Thatcher Government, 1979–83: Contemporary Conservatism and Economic Change*. Brighton: Wheatsheaf.
Horne, Alistair 1988: *Macmillan 1894–1956*. London: Macmillan.
Horne, Alistair 1989: *Macmillan 1957–1986*. London: Macmillan.
Howard, Anthony 1987: *RAB: The Life of R.A.Butler*. London: Cape.
Hurd, Douglas 1979: *An End to Promises*. London: Collins.
Ingham, Bernard 1991: *Kill the Messenger*. London: Harper Collins.
James, Robert Rhodes 1972: *Ambitions and Realities: British Politics 1964–70*. London: Weidenfeld & Nicolson.

James, Robert Rhodes 1986: *Anthony Eden*. London: Weidenfeld & Nicolson.

Jefferys, Kevin (ed.) 1987a: *Labour and the War time Coalition: From the Diary of James Chuter Ede 1941–1945*. London: Historians Press.

Jefferys, Kevin 1987b: British politics and Social Policy during the Second World War. *Historical Journal*, 30, pp. 123–44.

Jefferys, Kevin 1991: *The Churchill Coalition and War time Politics*. Manchester: Manchester University Press.

Jefferys, Kevin 1992: *The Attlee Government 1945–1951*. London: Longman.

Jefferys, Kevin 1993: *The Labour Party since 1945*. London: Macmillan.

Jenkins, Peter 1987: *Mrs Thatcher's Revolution: the Ending of the Socialist Era*. London: Cape.

Jenkins, Roy 1982: Home Thoughts from Abroad, in Kennet, Wayland (ed.), *The Rebirth of Britain*. London: Weidenfeld and Nicolson.

Jenkins, Roy 1991: *A Life at the Centre*. London: Macmillan.

Jones, Jack 1986: *Union Man*. London: Collins.

Jones, Tudor 1989: Is Labour Abandoning its Socialist Roots? *Contemporary Record*, 3, pp. 6–8.

Joseph, Sir Keith 1987: Escaping the Chrysalis of Statism. *Contemporary Record*, 1, pp. 26–31.

Kavanagh, Dennis 1987: *Thatcherism and British Politics: The End of Consensus?* Oxford: Oxford University Press.

Kavanagh, Dennis 1992: The Post-war Consensus. *Twentieth Century British History*, 3, pp. 175–90.

Kavanagh, Dennis and Morris, Peter 1989: *Consensus Politics from Attlee to Thatcher*. Oxford: Basil Blackwell.

Kavanagh, Dennis and Morris, Peter 1994: *Consensus Politics from Attlee to Major*. Oxford: Basil Blackwell.

Kavanagh, Dennis and Seldon, Anthony (eds) 1989: *The Thatcher Effect*. Oxford: Oxford University Press.

Kavanagh, Dennis and Seldon, Anthony (eds) 1994: *The Major Effect*. London: Macmillan.

Keegan, William 1989: *Mr. Lawson's Gamble*. London: Hodder and Stoughton.

Kellner, Peter 1989: Adapting to the Post war Consensus. *Contemporary Record*, 3, pp. 11–15.

Lamb, Richard 1987: *The Failure of the Eden Government*. London: Sidgwick & Jackson.

Lamb, Richard 1995: *The Macmillan Years 1957–1963*. London: John Murray.

Lapping, Brian 1985: *End of Empire*. London: Granada.

Lawson, Nigel 1992: *The View from No.11*. London: Bantam.

Letwin, Shirley 1992: *The Anatomy of Thatcherism*. London: Fontana.

Lindsay, T. F. and Harrington, Michael 1979: *The Conservative Party 1918–1979*. London: Macmillan.

Lowe, Rodney 1990a: The Second World War, Consensus and the Foundation of the Welfare State. *Twentieth Century British History*, 1, pp. 152–82.

Lowe, Rodney 1990b: Welfare Policy in Britain 1943–1970. *Contemporary Record*, 4, 2, pp. 29–32.

McKenzie, Robert 1955: *British Political Parties*. London: Heinemann.

Macmillan, Harold 1969: *Tides of Fortune 1945–55*. London: Macmillan.

Macmillan, Harold 1971: *Riding the Storm 1956–1959*. London: Macmillan.

Margach, James 1978: *The Abuse of Power*. London: W.H. Allen.

Marquand, David 1988: *The Unprincipled Society*. London: Cape.

Maudling, Reginald 1978: *Memoirs*. London: Sidgwick and Jackson.

Middlemas, Keith 1979: *Politics in Industrial Society: The Experience of the British System Since 1911*. London: Deutsch.

Middlemas, Keith 1986: *Power, Competition and the State: Britain in Search of Balance, 1940–61*. London: Macmillan.

Mikardo, Ian 1988: *Back-bencher*. London: Weidenfeld and Nicolson.

Miliband, Ralph 1973: *Parliamentary Socialism*. London: Merlin Press.

Morgan, Kenneth 1984: *Labour in Power 1945–51*. Oxford: Clarendon Press.

Morgan, Kenneth 1987: *Labour People*. Oxford: Oxford University Press.

Morgan, Kenneth 1988: Nationalisation and Privatisation. *Contemporary Record*, 2, pp. 32–4.

Morgan, Kenneth 1990: *The People's Peace: British History 1945–1990*. Oxford: Oxford University Press.

Muller, Christopher 1996: The Institute of Economic Affairs: Undermining the Post-war Consensus. *Contemporary British History*, 10, pp. 88–110.

Paterson, Peter 1993: *Tired and Emotional. The Life of Lord George Brown*. London: Chatto and Windus.

Peden, George 1985: *British Economic and Social Policy: Lloyd George to Margaret Thatcher*. Oxford: Phillip Allen.

Peden, George 1988: *Keynes, The Treasury and British Economic Policy*. London: Macmillan.

Pelling, Henry 1984: *The Labour Government 1945–51*. London: Macmillan.

Pimlott, Ben 1985: *Hugh Dalton*. London: Cape.

Pimlott, Ben (ed.) 1986a: *The Second World War Diary of Hugh Dalton.* London: Cape/London School of Economics.

Pimlott, Ben (ed.) 1986b: *The Political Diary of Hugh Dalton.* London: Cape/London School of Economics.

Pimlott, Ben 1988: The Myth of Consensus, in Smith, L. M. (ed.), *The Making of Britain: Echoes of Greatness.* London: Macmillan.

Pimlott, Ben 1989: Is Post war Consensus a Myth? *Contemporary Record,* 2, pp. 12–14.

Pimlott, Ben 1992: *Harold Wilson.* London: Harper Collins.

Ponting, Clive 1989: *Breach of Promise.* London: Hamish Hamilton.

Porter, Bernard 1994: *Britannia's Burden.* London: Edward Arnold.

Prior, James 1986: *A Balance of Power.* London: Hamilton.

Ramsden, John 1980: *The Making of Conservative Party Policy.* London: Longman.

Ramsden, John 1987: A Party for Owners or a Party for Earners. *Transactions of the Royal Historical Society,* 5th series, 37, pp. 49–63.

Ramsden, John 1995: *The Age of Churchill and Eden 1940–1957.* London: Longman.

Ramsden, John 1996: *The Winds of Change: Macmillan to Heath 1957–1975.* London: Longman.

Rentoul, John 1995: *Tony Blair.* London: Little, Brown and Company.

Riddell, Peter 1983: *The Thatcher Government.* Oxford: Martin Robertson.

Riddell, Peter 1993: Consensus, What Consensus. *The Times,* 12 April 1993.

Ridley, Nicholas 1991: *My Style of Government.* London: Hutchinson.

Robertson, David 1976: *A Theory of Party Competition.* London: Wiley.

Rollings, Neil 1988: British Budgetary Policy 1945–1954: A 'Keynesian Revolution'? *Economic History Review,* 41, pp. 283–98.

Rollings, Neil 1994: 'Poor Mr. Butskell: A Short Life, Wrecked by Schizophrenia'? *Twentieth Century British History,* 5, pp. 183–205.

Rose, Richard 1980: *Do Parties Make a Difference?* London: Macmillan.

Searle, Geoffrey 1995: *Country Before Party.* London: Longman.

Seldon, Anthony 1981: *Churchill's Indian Summer: The Conservative Government, 1951–55.* London: Hodder & Stoughton.

Seldon, Anthony 1994: The Rise and Fall (and rise again?) of the Post-war Consensus, in Jones, Bill et al. (eds), *Politics UK.* Hemel Hempstead: Harvester Wheatsheaf.

Seyd, Patrick 1987: *The Rise and Fall of the Labour Left.* London: Macmillan.

Shaw, Eric 1996: *The Labour Party since 1945.* Oxford: Blackwell Publishers.

Shepherd, Robert 1994: *Iain Macleod*. London: Hutchinson.

Sked, Alan and Cook, Chris 1979: *Post-War Britain: A Political History*. Brighton: Harvester.

Smith, Martin 1992: The Labour Party in Opposition, in Smith, M. and Spear, J. (eds), *The Changing Labour Party*. London: Routledge.

Sopel, Jon 1995: *Tony Blair, the Moderniser*. London: Michael Joseph.

Steel, David 1980: *A House Divided: The Lib–Lab Pact and the Future of British Politics*. London: Weidenfeld & Nicolson.

Taylor, Robert 1989: Mrs Thatcher's Impact on the TUC. *Contemporary Record*, 2, pp. 23–6.

Taylor, Robert 1993: *The Trade Union Question in British Politics*. Oxford: Blackwell.

Tebbit, Norman 1988: *Upwardly Mobile*. London: Weidenfeld and Nicolson.

Tebbit, Norman 1991: *Unfinished Business*. London: Weidenfeld and Nicolson.

Thatcher, Margaret 1993: *The Downing Street Years*. London: Harper Collins.

Thatcher, Margaret 1995: *The Path to Power*. London: HarperCollins.

Thorpe, D. R. 1989: *Selwyn Lloyd*. London: Cape.

Tiratsoo, Nick (ed.) 1991: *The Attlee Years*. London: Pinter.

Walker, Peter 1977: *The Ascent of Britain*. London: Sidgwick and Jackson.

Whitehead, Phillip 1985: *The Writing on the Wall*. London: Michael Joseph.

Whitelaw, William 1989: *The Whitelaw Memoirs*. London: Aurum.

Williams, Philip 1979: *Hugh Gaitskell: A Political Biography*. London: Cape.

Williams, Philip (ed.) 1983: *The Diary of Hugh Gaitskell 1945–1956*. London: Cape.

Wilson, Harold 1979: *Final Term: The Labour Government 1974–1976*. London: Weidenfeld & Nicolson.

Wilton, Iain 1990: Postwar Consensus. *Contemporary Record*, 3, 4, pp. 27–8.

Woolton, Lord 1959: *Memoirs*. London: Cassell.

Wyatt, Woodrow 1977: *What's Left of the Labour Party*. London: Sidgwick and Jackson.

Young, Hugo 1989: *One of Us*. London: Macmillan.

Young, Kenneth (ed.) 1980: *The Diaries of Sir Robert Bruce Lockhart 1939–1965*. London: Macmillan.

Ziegler, Philip 1993: *Harold Wilson*. London: Weidenfeld and Nicolson.

Index